Golf
STORIES
& JOKES
for Speakers

BRIDE: Whatever made you bring your silly old golf clubs to our wedding?

GROOM: Well, it's not going to take all day, is it?

Golf STORIES & JOKES for Speakers

Compiled by
Geoffrey Matson

foulsham

LONDON · NEW YORK · TORONTO · SYDNEY

foulsham

Bennetts Close, Cippenham, Berks. SL1 5AP

ISBN 0–572–01605–0

Copyright © 1990 Geoffrey J. Matson
Originally published as *Off The Tee*

Printed and bound in Great Britain by
Cox & Wyman Ltd, Reading, Berkshire

*This book is dedicated to my nephew Malcolm,
who, although he lives within a short distance
of the Wentworth Course and has visited it
on a number of occasions, still prefers rowing
to playing golf – the clot!*

ACKNOWLEDGEMENTS

My grateful thanks go to all those, whose names are listed on the following pages, who have helped so willingly in providing the material which has made this miscellany possible. I am also grateful for the particular and varied help they have given to the British Broadcasting Corporation, Professional Golfers' Association, Bert Aza Agency Ltd., George Bartram Press Relations Organization, David Coleman, *Country Life*, The George Cohen 600 Group Ltd. and Exclusive Press Features Ltd. I must also thank my wife and secretary, without whose cheerful and untiring assistance in collecting and arranging these contributions, my task would have been so much harder.

G. J. Matson.

CONTENTS

Golf STORIES & JOKES
for Speakers

Foreword

Golf is a very fascinating game; and those who play it, particularly the ones who take it seriously, never tire of talking about it. Come up to a crowd of players at the 'nineteenth' – which, for the uninitiated, is the title affectionately given to the Clubhouse – and you will almost invariably find a lot of excited chatter. One group may be going through the game they have just played, analysing it shot by shot; another group will be listening to a player describing a good shot which he has played recently and of which he is very proud; a third group may be holding an inquest on one or two bad strokes and trying to find out what went wrong; whilst in a corner, grasping their tankards of beer, two or three fellows are probably swopping golf stories and punctuating their conversation at varying intervals with hearty guffaws of laughter.

There are probably more good stories connected with golf than with any other game. This is due mainly, I believe, to the fact that most comedians and people interested in entertaining generally are keen golfers. When these folk get together, they are always exchanging stories; and amusing incidents, and flashes of wit, which crop up unexpectedly during play, are soon enlarged into good stories. Moreover, by the very nature of their calling, these folk are able to remember stories longer than most of us. Whenever I have approached an entertainer who plays golf himself, it has not taken him long to give me two or three good stories.

When you come to think of it, I suppose, golfers themselves are really rather funny folk. In any case, much of their language, and many of their actions must often appear queer to the average person. When they go out to play they often talk about driving off but invariably finish up by walking; they get a caddie to set up a tee and then leave the tee and go off with the caddie; and whilst the majority of them are undoubtedly truthful and upright citizens, not one would deny that he, or she, prefers a good lie. They curse because they have sliced a ball but when eventually they find it, if ever they do, it is invariably found to be in perfect condition. They can halve a hole, still leave it whole, and finally finish the round all square. Often, however, they say they have finished when actually there are still three or four more holes to play. A player can go down in one and finish one up. If they ever are lucky enough to hole out in one nobody ever buys them a drink in recognition of a wonderful achievement; instead, it usually costs them five quid or more in the Clubhouse for being so darned clever! And finally, even Solomon in all *his* glory was not arrayed like some I have known.

I have been surprised at the relatively few occasions on which a story has been duplicated. A few, of course, have been given to me by more than one person and when this has happened, I have selected the version I like best and given credit for it as well to the others who supplied it. Thus, for example, there is one story for which credit has been given to Sir Geoffrey Barnett, Franklin Engelmann and Leslie Crowther. The version I have used was that given me by Sir Geoffrey Barnett and with this particular story, I was very amused to find how the clergyman who forms the subject of it, changed his religious convictions so readily. In one version he was a Presbyterian, in another an Anglican, and he finished up finally as a Rabbi!

When I first thought of compiling this book, I intended filling it entirely with stories. Some of the people I approached, however, preferred to describe a personal golfing experience or contribute a short piece on golf in general. Arthur Askey has supplied an amusing account of his connections with golf: Bing Crosby has recorded the peculiar comments made by officials sent to inspect a Course in Austria; Sydney Spicer, well known sports writer, has described some unusual golfing feats; Peter Haigh gives details of an interesting and unique Golf Club which he founded in conjunction with McDonald Hobley; Stanley Unwin has contributed a piece in the kind of language which only he can produce and for which he has become so popular; Dai Rees describes a marathon match which he once played against Jerry Barber from Los Angeles and makes some interesting comments on American golf in general, whilst Bernard Hunt has contributed an interesting and practical piece on 'The Art of Practising'.

Thus the book has turned into a miscellany of golfing pieces of all kinds, and as you flick through the following pages, I think you may find much in them to give you enjoyment. I hope you will.

Geoffrey J. Matson.

The American Approach

One of the most remarkable matches in which I ever played took place in front of television cameras – and lasted for ten hours!

The venue was a windy and rainswept West Course at Wentworth Golf Club in Surrey (the 'Burma Road'), the prize money was 5,000 dollars and my opponent was the gnome-like Jerry Barber, forty-five-year-old professional from Los Angeles. It was 1961, and later in the year both of us were to lead our respective countries in another Ryder Cup encounter.

Perhaps I had better explain that ten hours! We were playing the match for the U.S. television film, and the cameras and other production equipment had to be moved around the course between every shot!

It was the longest single match in which I had played, but it gave me a close-up of the American approach to golf and this was an experience, even though I had seen plenty of it internationally in the past.

Jerry never smiled once during our clash – and he never missed a putt. Even by American standards he is a world-class performer on the greens and it seemed that no matter how far off-target he was with his long shots, the pin-point accurate recovery was always well within him.

That, of course, is typically American. Their golfers have this motto: 'Drive for show, and putt for dough!'

Let me give you an example of the typical American four. At the first tee Barber shaped up for his drive and promptly hooked the ball way off to the left past Tom Haliburton's professional's shop and into the base of the trees and shrubs off the fairway.

It looked six to me, for that first hole demands a big shot across a steep valley and uphill to the green. It didn't worry Barber unduly. He lashed the ball out to the bottom of the valley, smacked it up on to the edge of the green, and ran down a single putt from sixteen feet!

Not a trace of emotion! He walked on to the second tee – a short hole – and drove his tee shot neatly into a bunker. This time he blasted out ten feet from the flag and holed it for a par three.

At times during this long round, and without wishing to appear immodest, I marvelled that this amazing man was not half a dozen shots behind me. But he was never more than three, and after fourteen holes I had another taste of this fearless American determination not to give up.

On the fifteenth tee I told two friends: 'If I can hold Jerry on the next two I think I've got him'. Well, he got one stroke back at the fifteenth after a sliced drive, and snatched another at the long seventeenth.

At the home hole, he was pin-high to the left while I was messing about among the roots of a large beech some forty yards short of the green. The TV director was alerting his camera crew and telling them to get ready to 'roll it'. He checked with me whether this was all right. I told him: 'You just keep 'em rolling for a while – I'll give it a knock in a minute'.

I pulled out my best shot of the match, reached the edge of the green and Jerry and I each took five. He was so surprised that I had managed to get clear of the dead leaves and branches that he chipped up fifteen feet short – his only ill-judged short stroke of the match. I won the game by one stroke!

Dai Rees.
(Four times British Ryder Cup Captain)

Two Reverend Gentlemen

I suppose I know scores of golfing stories but two of the many which have caused me most amusement are the following:

The first concerns a 'Major' type who was renowned for his fruity language. Going out to play one day he was approached by the secretary who said, 'I hope you don't mind my mentioning this, sir, but there are a couple of clergymen out on the course today so *do* be careful of your language.' The man grunted and went out to play – some time later returning and buttonholing the secretary. 'What do you mean, "clergymen",' he shouted. 'I saw one of them in a bunker and I have never heard such dreadful language in all my life – are you sure they are clergymen?' 'Well, there's the visitors' book,' said the secretary, 'look for yourself.' And there in the book the man read, 'A. Jones and B. Williams – *Metropolitan Vickers*'.

*   *   *

Another story I find amusing is this one. A certain member brought a visitor to his course one Saturday morning and the few members gathered on the first tee asked them to play first as a courtesy to the visitor. The latter teed up his ball and after a couple of practice swings walked up to the ball and gave a mighty lunge at it, missing it by quite a margin. This happened four times in rapid succession when the perspiring visitor, seeing the looks of horror he was getting from the members, gave a sheepish grin and said, 'You see – *my* course is about three inches *higher* than this.'

Ted Ray.

An Awkward Dilemma

The captain of a Golf Club and a new member were badly held up by two ladies hacking away in a bunker ahead. 'Tell them to let us through,' said the new member. The captain walked towards the ladies but returned before long and said

'Sorry, old boy, I couldn't tell them to move on – you see, one of them is my wife and the other is my girl-friend.'

'Then let me try,' said the new member. He too returned without having had any success and said to the captain, 'I couldn't ask them to move either – for the same reason!'

McDonald Hobley.

Snake in the Hole

This is rather an amusing experience I had when on the Australian Tour in 1959.

On the beautiful Hume Wood golf course at Port Elizabeth, we had the opportunity of playing a round during matches. The course has a reputation for the large number of snakes that seem to live among the undergrowth and can even be found on the greens.

Denis Compton and Godfrey Evans were following our four round when we came upon a dead snake lying on the third green – a green which was hidden from the fairway by some trees. When we had played our hole, Godfrey Evans had the bright idea of putting the dead snake in the hole and a few moments afterwards a ball landed on the green from the following pair who were still out of sight. Godfrey nipped smartly on to the green, put the ball on top of the snake, and we continued. When they arrived on the green the players were completely mystified by the disappearance of the ball and then staggered to find it in the hole with the snake!

We played on, and it was several days before a word was said about the brilliant second shot which holed out on top of the snake – they weren't sure whether to brag or to pretend it never happened!

Colin Cowdrey.

The World's Worst Golfer

To all poor and distressed golfers – wherever they may be. Although I am undoubtedly the best comedian in the country, I am probably the world's worst golfer. Me, wot's been president and captain of the Stage Golfing Society, and a member of the Vaudeville and Concert Golfing Societies, and a golfer of thirty years standing. My official handicap is sixteen, off the ladies' tee. I played last year with a member of the Vaudeville Golfing Society who I thought was about my weight. Our opponents were Dai Rees and Bernard Hunt. After a couple of holes, they started giving my partner little hints but me they ignored. They could see the hopelessness of it all. Yet, apart from lifting my head, jumping off my feet, coming through like lightning and shanking, I think I have quite a classic style. I refuse to sacrifice my style for distance anyway. My boomerang drive is the talk of all the Golf Clubs where I play. I drive well out to the left and it's a joy to see the ball coming back into the centre of the fairway. Of course I occasionally hit a straight one and that doesn't half mess me up. But I'm very good at keeping the score. With members of the Vaudeville Golfing Society you need to be! I played a fellow last week – a liar if ever there was one – and I knew he was cheating about the number of strokes he had taken . . . he said he'd won the hole. Anyway I went carefully through the shots we had taken, and he had to agree that we had halved – in 23!

I won't attempt to tell you any golfing stories – the other comics in this book will have told them – but let me assure you that all the really funny ones are mine! But I do hope that Ted Ray has told the true one of his – when there were tremendous excavations going on alongside a well-known golf course – and Ted strolled over to the foreman and said, 'Was it a new one?' I wish I'd said it. I probably will some time.

So to all golfers I say, 'Ahno fiz shomlem si farzim.' I don't

know what it means but it's what the Bishop said when he hit
his shin with his niblick.

Arthur Askey.

'Golf'

Golf! What is it that draws us to it? We play it, some of us
hate it, others dislike it, more like it, others love it and some
are captivated by it. Very few are indifferent. Why? This is a
question that has been asked since the game began, and nobody
has yet produced a satisfactory answer. I certainly wouldn't pre-
sume to advance a reason, but a few ideas have been put forward
by various people, so here they are, and the reader can judge for
himself.

One theory – a Freudian one for what it is worth – is that man
in striding around, hitting a golf ball, is satisfying some deep
primeval jungle instinct. Instead of chasing through the forest,
with not much on but a piece of cloth in the right place, and
hunting animals with bow and arrow, he puts on plus-fours
and beats a golf ball all over the countryside in order to satisfy
some complex, unfathomable desires. A strange idea – there
might be something in it though – I know when I can put it
over someone (it doesn't happen all that often) I dislike intensely,
to the tune of six and four, I do satisfy something.

Another theory – I rather go for this one – is that golf is like
a mistress; beautiful, provocative, beloved and tempting always.
We love her but hate her at the same time; we try to conquer
her, but she will not be conquered, and yet she is always tempting
us to try again, and try again we do. We believe some happy
precious times that we have captured her secret, but still alluring
and always tempting she quickly draws away, but never so far
that we will not make another attempt to capture that precious
citadel.

I remember once talking to a clever distinguished Q.C., who, in the few moments of relaxation he was able to take from his busy profession, played a hard enthusiastic game of golf to eight handicap. I asked him why he thought so many able, brainy, determined men were so devoted to the game of golf. He replied, 'I think deep down that they have the same instincts as Mallory, who, when asked why he wanted to climb Mount Everest, replied "Because it's there". They know very well that they will never conquer it, but that doesn't stop them trying.'

His answer reminded me of a gentleman I once knew at a provincial club in Yorkshire. A strange, gruff, taciturn fellow of sixty odd, he had the reputation of having been a secret service agent. I was told by his associates that a retired secret service agent must never disclose that he has been one or he forfeits his pension. This retired gentleman led a strange golfing life; every mid-week afternoon, he would arrive at the Golf Club at precisely two o'clock, take out exactly a dozen golf balls and three clubs, never more and never less, to one of the remoter fairways. He would hit these balls up and down the fairway for exactly one hour and forty-five minutes and then return to the Clubhouse, where he would have his tea served to him at four o'clock. His routine never varied and at half past four he would return to his home. I was a schoolboy at the time and occasionally used to watch him practise. He would hit a dozen brassie shots in succession, virtually dead straight about 180 yards, and would have played to about six handicap had he cared to indulge much in games. It was a rare occasion when anyone could tempt him out for a game, though very occasionally he could be persuaded to play nine holes at the week-end – but never mid-week; that would have interfered with his practice.

I became friendly with him – about as friendly as anyone could be with this silent, retiring fellow. Whilst on holiday, I would often talk with him. One mid-week afternoon I came across him having his tea in the Club lounge, and went over to have a chat. I noticed that he was unnaturally elated as he motioned to me to sit down. He waited until I was comfortable and then announced in pontifical manner, 'I have discovered the secret of the game of golf, I shall never hit a bad shot again.' He said that he had played golf all his life, but had only had the opportunity to concentrate seriously on it for the last five years, and now at last he had found the answer. I remember feeling somewhat sceptical, although only a schoolboy, that anyone could have found the key to this mysterious game. Unfortunately, before he had time to elaborate on his discovery, it was time for him to catch his bus.

The next afternoon I was told by the steward at the Club that during the night he had died peacefully in his sleep of a heart attack. Whilst feeling sad at his loss, I could not help thinking rather wistfully how lucky he was. He had died just after the discovery of the enigma for which he had been searching all his life. I have often thought of this since and realized his great good fortune. Not for him the disillusionment on the morrow or even the bitterness of an end achieved.

Why are golf devotees so utterly fascinated by it? Who knows! Is it that 'Dear Octopus' which binds us with its loving but unbreakable tentacles? Perhaps we should just accept its bewitching hold and leave it at that.

Onlooker ('Golfing').

Poor Caddie!

I'm afraid the world has not seen a more completely non-golf person than myself. The game is an absolutely closed book to me and I would not even know which end to swing a caddie.

So golfing reminiscences are out, and as for golfing jokes – well, I can never understand them so I would not dare to tell one.

Denis Norden.

Some Quickies

There are scores of golfing quips which have made me smile at one time or another. Here are a few of the ones I can remember just now.

'Well, caddie, I guess I'm about the worst golfer in the world.'

'Oh, no, sir, there are a lot worse than you but they don't play.'

*   *   *

'So the judge fined you fifty dollars for hitting your wife with a club?'

'Oh, it wasn't so much for hitting her as it was for using the wrong club.'

*   *   *

'Do you think it's a sin for me to play golf on Sunday?'

'The way you play – it's a sin to play golf any day.'

*   *   *

'Murphy got rich quick, didn't he?'

'He got rich so quick that he can't swing a golf club without spitting on his hands.'

*   *   *

'Say, caddie, why do you keep looking at your watch?'

'It isn't a watch, sir, it's a compass.'

*   *   *

'There is a new dictionary for golfing terms just out.'

'Well, if it's complete it will be banned.'

*   *   *

'Your trouble is that you don't address the ball properly.'

'Well, I was polite to the darn thing as long as possible.'

*   *   *

GOLFER: Why do you keep looking at your watch?
CADDIE: It isn't a watch, sir, it's a compass.

'How's your daughter's golf?'
'She says she is going round in less and less every day.'
'I don't doubt that, but I asked about her golf.'

*   *   *

'My wife says if I don't chuck golf, she'll leave me.'
'I say – hard luck.'
'Ye-es – I'll miss her.'

*   *   *

'You think so much of your old golf game that you don't even remember when we were married.'
'Of course I do, my dear, it was the day I sank that thirty-foot putt.'

*   *   *

'Well, how do you like my game?'
'I suppose it's all right, but I still prefer golf.'

Wilfred Pickles.

An Erring Minister

A Scottish minister, whose Manse garden ran down to the third tee of a golf course, woke very early one beautiful Sunday morning and looked out on to the course shimmering in the sunshine. Temptation overcame him, and, stealing out, he collected his clubs and went to the third tee.

But above, St. Peter saw what he was about and went to the Lord and said, 'Lord, do you see the minister playing on the Sabbath? Shall I send a thunderbolt to chasten him?'

The Lord replied, 'Leave him to me, Peter.'

The minister teed up and drove straight and clean down the middle of the fairway – the ball popped over the edge of the green and landed in the hole.

Appalled, Peter turned to the Lord and said, 'Lord, I thought you were going to chasten him.'

To which the Lord replied, 'I have, Peter, I have – whom can he tell?'

Sir Geoffrey Barnett.
Franklin Engelmann.
Leslie Crowther.

Officialdom Gone Mad

I was in the Austrian Tyrol a year or two ago, at Kitzbuhel, where three or four years ago some dedicated souls, against all kinds of natural impediments, designed and constructed a golf course. I must tell you it is rather a nice nine-hole course, with beautiful vistas in every direction.

Before the formal opening it was necessary to get official approval of the provincial government, and a three man committee for that purpose came down to Kitzbuhel from Innsbruck.

But formidable difficulties arose. One of the committee carried a skull which he tapped with a golf ball, demonstrating the lethal effects of a direct hit. The second fellow was against the project because, as he said, having the horses charging up and down all over the countryside was a menace to pedestrians, cattle and sheep. But the chairman of the group was most adamant. 'Why,' he exclaimed, 'these people here have asked approval for one golf course. They've already built nine, and they're talking about another nine in a couple of years!'

Bing Crosby.

Playing for a Drink

A keen golfing parson was asked by the Club steward to give a stranger a game. He immediately agreed and they set out to play. The first remark the stranger made when they reached the first tee, was, 'What shall we play for?' 'I always play for fun,' said the parson.

'That's a bit dull,' replied the stranger. 'Let's play for drinks.'

The parson hesitated and hedged a little, but not wishing to appear unfriendly he eventually agreed. They played the round and the stranger won easily. Back in the Clubhouse, the parson said, 'I'll keep my promise; what will you have?'

'A bottle of whisky, please,' said the stranger.

Hearing this the parson winced and turned a trifle pale but he felt that, having made a bargain, he must keep to it. He asked the barman to give the stranger a bottle and he paid for it.

During the conversation which followed the stranger learned that the parson's church was not far from where he lived. 'I should like to come and hear you preach one day,' he said. 'I'll arrange that and bring my father and mother along with me,' he added.

'That's a very good idea,' said the parson. 'You bring your father and mother along – and I'll be pleased *to marry them*.'

Anon.

The Art of Practising

Practice makes perfect is an old and very true saying. But to get the full benefit from practice you should try to work to a method or routine. It is often a waste of effort to go out on to the fairway with a huge bag of balls, take out your driver and slog away into the far distance until you are exhausted. Many times I have heard the complaint, 'I'm worse after practice,' and that is why.

I have found through experience that the best way to improve your game and also to get the most enjoyment from practising, is to have not more than three dozen or so balls, pick a target and then start off with the short clubs. A hill, a small tree, or even a tuft of grass will do, and then try and group the balls as near as possible to this target, making sure that you're not having to hit too hard at the ball to get it there. A three-quarter swing gives greater accuracy and better feel for range or distance. As you work up through the clubs, try to visualize imaginary problems – a tree in the way so that you must hit the ball a little higher, a wind against so this one must be a little lower, and so on. Try to play each shot separately, thinking over each one and don't just practise aimlessly. This will get you nowhere, as your interest will soon fade and very shortly after that your patience. Above all, guard against the greatest temptation which is to hit the next one a little farther than the last. This creeps in without realizing it, and then the wild shots start. This is the time to go back to the short clubs again.

I find that one of the most enjoyable and profitable parts of the game to practise is pitching. If you can, pitch on to a green and this time take only a dozen or so balls. Play from just off the green and then try to hole as many putts as possible. It's amazing how the one-chip percentage goes up, and this is the thing that counts on those Sunday morning four-balls.

Above all, don't overdo the practice. One hour when you are fresh, with plenty of thought and concentration, is worth ten of gruelling work when you are tired.

Bernard Hunt.

Fore !

At a Pro-celebrity match recently, I partnered Ruiz, the Argentinian. I am not qualified really to carry his clubs. At the first, in front of a big gallery, I was duly announced, and subsequently missed the ball on the tee shot. Everyone thought I was being funny since I am known somewhat as a bit of a lad.

The second attempt, however, almost killed some of the gallery. There was no more laughter then, as they realized that I was a very nervous actor, trying to *look* like a golfer.

Leslie Phillips.

Delayed Instruction

A newly rich Jewish gentleman decided to take up golf and went to the local professional and arranged to have lessons. The first day on the first tee he took his very first smack at a ball and put it right on the green!

'*Very* good, Mr. Goldberg,' said the professional, 'now we take a walk up to the green and carry on.'

'Carry on?' said Mr. Goldberg.

'Yes,' said the professional, 'now we have to get the ball into the little hole.'

At this Mr. Goldberg looked very annoyed and said, '*Now* you tell me.'

Sidney James.

The 'Haho' Golf Club

McDonald Hobley and I have been chums for many years and have been playing golf together for a considerable time. One day it occurred to us that there may well be a lot of people, both in show business and out, whose love of the game and whose sheer enjoyment could be turned to a charitable use, several times a year.

With this in mind, we formed a Club called HAHO (being the first two initial letters of *Haigh* and *Hobley*). Since this Club is rather unique I am thinking that details of it may interest many of your readers. Our motto is 'Ludendo Alios Sublevamus', which being freely translated means, 'By playing among ourselves, we help others'.

To further explain the distribution of monies raised, I would tell you that each member of the HAHO Organization is, in turn, given the proceeds of each quarterly match and invited to distribute the money as they see fit, particularly to old folks or deserving single causes. In fact, to anybody to whom £50, £100 or £150 could mean the difference between misery and happiness.

These are our rules:

1. Membership is by invitation and will be strictly limited.
2. There are no subscriptions.
3. The Club will play a minimum of four money raising matches a year, one of which will be among *members only* for the Club Trophy, the 'Haho', and called Haho Day. Three matches will be played roughly every quarter and all monies raised, by any means, fair, foul or exclusive, at each match, will be given to members in rotation for charitable distribution at their discretion.
4. The playing fee for each quarterly match will be £2 exclusive of all other expenses. If a member is unable to be present at a match he is required to send an 'absence' fee of £1 towards the fund. Each quarterly fund is to be donated on behalf of Haho to any charitable or deserving cause that the respective member thinks fit.

   Haho insists that the money be devoted to a person or cause to whom a few pounds will mean a great deal. They do not want the money to be absorbed into a nationally supported organization.
5. *The 'Haho'*. The holder of the 'Haho' is to nominate the course on which he will defend his title and will act as secretary for the match. He will also nominate match secretaries for the three other matches played during his term.
6. *Uniform*. The Haho uniform *must* be worn at all Haho matches.

It consists of Oxford blue trousers, Cambridge blue sweater and shirt, and Oxford blue cap bearing the Haho roundel.

All the above clothing is available at Simpsons.

(The cap is optional, but if one is worn it must be a Haho cap.)

7. The Haho tie is available at Simpsons.
8. The golfing term pin-high is not used by Haho during their matches. Instead the exultant shout or stimulating cry 'Orificisir' will be used.
9. *Sconces*. (These apply only to Haho Days and Match Days.)
   A. Incorrect dress – on Haho Days – fined one stroke from handicap.

   On Match Days – fined £10.
   B. Using the term pin-high by mistake – £5.
   C. Failure to wear Haho tie at meals in Clubhouse – £5.

   (All sconces to be added to the quarterly fund.)
10. There are no councils or committees in Haho and any decisions or matters of policy are the responsibility of the founders, McDonald Hobley and Peter Haigh, who shall be known as the Bogeymen.

Peter Haigh.

'I'm Tickled to Death, Missus'

To use a gag I generally include in my act, 'I'm tickled to death, missus', when I think of this little story. John Brown's friends were always telling him he was too fat to play golf but he didn't believe it until he started. Then he became convinced as he found that when he put the ball where he could see it he couldn't hit it, and when he put it where he could hit it he couldn't see it! Are you tickled, missus? I bet *he* was!

*   *   *

'Poor old Brown, when he puts the ball where he can see it, he can't hit it, and when he puts it where he can hit it, he can't see it.'

I was in a friend's house one day when he came home from golf, put his clubs in the hall, and then came on into the lounge, rubbing his hands and looking very cheerful.

'I had a marvellous round, darling,' he said. 'I must tell you about it.'

'All right,' said his wife sweetly, 'take off your boots and start with your drive at the eighteenth tee.'

*　　　*　　　*

And this is another story I think is funny. A golfer, who was not very good, took a caddie and went off round the course. The farther he got, the worse he got, and the caddie got more and more fed up. As they came to the eighteenth he heaved a sigh of relief, and then the golfer, smiling all over his face, turned to him and said: 'You perhaps won't believe it but I once did this hole in one.' The caddie, a poker-like expression on his face, looked up and merely said, 'Stroke or day, sir?'

Ken Dodd.

A Story of Courage on the Golf Course

The Second World War was over when, in the summer of 1947, the thoughts of all sportsmen returned to the games they had loved and given up in September 1939. So far as golfers were concerned, the British Isles were the holders of the Walker Cup which they won for the first and only time in 1938, and many of us learned with great pleasure that the United States were anxious to resume the series that very summer. It was our turn to go to America but since there were no funds in the Royal and Ancient till, the Americans very generously offered to come here and play the match at St. Andrews. I was one of a number of others who had played in the victorious side in 1938 and was highly delighted to be selected again for the match after a series of exhausting trials at St. Andrews in May. Three

GOLFER: You perhaps won't believe it, but I once did this hole in one.
CADDIE: Stroke or day, sir?

days later we faced the Americans, as usual a most formidable team, over the Old Course.

I think it is natural that everyone playing in this premier International feels a certain anxiety about his partner in the foursomes. For my part, as a distinctly poor putter, I was anxious to be given as a partner one of the best exponents of the art in our side, and the reader may well imagine my dismay when John Beck, our captain, informed me that he wished me to play with P. B. Lucas, the brilliant left-hander, whom I regarded as an extremely mediocre performer on the putting greens. However, there was nothing for it but to get down to some hard practice together and see how we could best play the course.

For the Open Championship of 1939 there had been made at the fourteenth a new back tee which had rendered that hole among the most difficult par fives in the world. Almost in every wind those terrifying pits known as the 'Beardies' in the middle of the fourteenth fairway now came into play and to my mind this hole was one of vital importance. I had evolved a method of playing it in 1939 which had worked out very well in the Open Championship and I, therefore, was most anxious to hit the tee shot at that hole in the Walker Cup foursomes. For this reason I suggested to Lucas, before we played our first practice round, that I should drive at the even holes. To my great surprise he said he particularly wanted to drive at the even holes himself and we therefore agreed to play the course either way in our two practice rounds. My method of playing the terrifying tee shot to the fourteenth was – regardless of wind – to hit straight at the 'Beardies' with a club with which one could not possibly reach them. I used to play the second shot over on to the fifth fairway leaving a third of no great difficulty or distance to the green. I explained this to Lucas and he seemed to think the method was a very good one. But, when he got up to the fourteenth tee in our first practice round, I noticed him hesitating in the distance and eventually changing an iron club for a wooden one. With this, as a left-hander, he hooked out of bounds, put down another, and with the same club hit it plumb into the 'Beardies'. His indecision alarmed me, and after the round I again approached him with a view to persuading him to allow me to drive at the even holes. He made the excuse that as a left-hander he did not wish to have to play the tee shot at the famous short eleventh and so, for the time being, I agreed to leave things as they were.

After further consideration I had another talk to him the next morning, pointing out that I felt the fourteenth was going to be the most critical hole and could lose us or win us the match over thirty-six holes, so in our final practice round he agreed to drive at the odd holes. I remember very little about this round save for the fact that he came to see me in my bedroom that evening and poured out the feelings of his driven mind.

He had been one of the most highly successful of our fighter pilots during the war and first made his name in command of a Canadian Squadron that saved Malta in the most critical year. To my amazement, he asked me whether after all I would agree to driving at the odd holes against America next day. This brave man explained to me that he was frightened of the ordeal ahead of him and that he did not feel confident of even hitting the ball in front of 5,000 people on the first tee next morning. I naturally agreed to change our plan, particularly in view of his assurance that after a couple of holes he would get over his fright.

I was very glad to release him from his obligation, but before going to sleep that evening I felt very depressed, since I had long ago made up my mind that there was only one possible way of facing first-class Americans over thirty-six holes and that was to play every hole from the first as though it were the last.

Everyone is nervous on these great occasions and some more so than others. My own feelings were indescribable as Lucas and I stepped on the first tee against Marvin Ward and Smiley Quick, one of the fiercest and toughest foursome pairings that ever represented America. Each subsequently lost his amateur status and I do not think that either ever had any real credentials as an amateur.

Though feeling the strain, my eye was 'in' and I lashed the first tee shot some ten yards short of the burn and that was a very great relief. The reader may well imagine one's dismay when my partner with a wedge, only moved our second shot a matter of two yards. I then, with trembling hands, managed to coax our ball up a yard from the hole and Lucas looking a little pale, failed to get a touch with his putt. One down already, and worse was to come, for Lucas topped his tee shot to the second hole. In this desperate situation the fates were kind to me since I lashed out with a wooden club and though I did not hit the ball truly, it finished twelve yards from the hole. Lucas hit our first putt five yards the other side of the hole and we were two down. I remember very little about the details of the next three holes save that we scrambled halves at the third and fourth in par figures and that after a very poor third by me at the long fifth, Lucas ran down a vast putt of about twenty yards to win the hole. Raymond Oppenheimer, one of our selectors who was inside the ropes observed, 'Boys, you are off now,' and how right he was so far as Lucas was concerned. By the turn, we were three up and I shall never forget the brilliance of his play or the courage of his putting. One shot stands out in particular, namely his No. 2 iron into a cross wind to the thirteenth hole. It finished a foot from the flag. On the fourteenth tee he took one look at the small gap between the 'Beardies' and the grey stone wall with 'out of bounds' beyond, and he hit, perhaps, the finest tee shot of his life.

We finished the round four up and much heartened. After lunch Ward and Quick, two of the most tenacious Americans ever to have represented the United States, hung on like limpets, and they got one hole back by the turn. There followed a most critical eleventh hole. Here the Americans got a two and Lucas, faced with a curly six-footer across that terrifying slope for a half,

39

put it down like a hero. The crisis was over. Lucas again hit his second with a long iron at the thirteenth right up against the flag, and with the Americans in the 'Beardies' from the fourteenth tee, all was over. Colonel Jack Inglis, our referee and not usually an emotional figure, burst into tears over his whisky and soda in the Clubhouse half an hour later, declaring that after that frightful start he did not believe that any human being had it in him to play like Lucas on that memorable day.

Leonard Crawley.

Tossing a Coin

Two golfers were talking together and one said he was often in a quandary not knowing quite what to do.

'What's the trouble?' asked the other.

'Well, I sometimes cannot make up my mind whether to play golf, whether to go fishing, or whether to stop at home with the missus.'

'Funny you should mention that. I had the same trouble myself at one time but I found a way of solving it.'

'Really, what do you do?'

'I always spin a coin. If it comes down heads I play golf, if it comes down tails I go fishing, but if it stands up on its end, I stop at home with the missus.'

Morecambe and Wise.

Holes-in-One – and Other Freaks

I once heard a story about the late J. W. H. T. Douglas, a controversial personality noted more for his exploits as a Test cricketer and Olympic middleweight boxing champion than for his golf.

It seems he was invariably struggling on the golf course and John Douglas had no time for failure. On one occasion, when his game was falling apart, he reached the limit of endurance after hitting one ball and then another into a lake. The story goes that without a word he relieved his caddie of the clubs, returned his driver to the bag and tossed them into the water too before stalking straight back to the Clubhouse.

Doubtless on his grim walk-in, he would have endorsed in acid terms the view of another frustrated golfer who proclaimed that not even a woman is as unpredictable as a flaming golf ball.

Certainly it travels farther (the golf ball I mean) and it disappears more readily than any piece of sporting ammunition other than that which is fired from a gun. All manner of freakish results follow the endeavours of millions of addicts to control its flight and its behaviour on landing.

The most popular and most proudly recalled of all freak shots is, of course, the tee shot which holes out in one. In theory it is the acme of perfection. In fact it is a sheer fluke, though the joy of its achievement is never allowed to be dimmed by this candid assessment.

The hole-in-one by even the humblest of players in the most casual of rounds, is guaranteed a brief acclaim in print. At the other end of the scale an American tournament professional can earn as much as £17,800 for doing it in a major event. Three of them, Don January, Joe Campbell and Dick Mayer have so enriched themselves with one single swing of a golf club.

Personally, I have never been able to understand all the fuss with which the feat is heralded. To date I have done it only once – and that in a county match when the subsequent excitement among a group of experienced players tickled me more than the success of the tee shot. Quite definitely I have had bigger thrills from the game. Every bit as satisfying were the several occasions on which, thanks to a similarly generous ration of luck, I have holed out second shots varying in length from a full spoon to a nine-iron pitch.

These flukes, each resulting from a ball played where I found it lying and not teed up on a selected spot – and therefore in theory more difficult – never brought so much as a flicker of an eye-brow from anyone. Clearly the significance of the whole thing is the scoring of a one at a par three hole, not a two at a hole of possibly 400 yards plus, which may even be a five on the card.

The fact of having achieved the distinction can be a useful string to your bow at those formal introductions where names pass into one ear and out through the other as fast as the swish of a golf club. However, in the small talk which follows, 'Have you ever holed in one?' is by way of being the stock banality put by the non-golfer to the golfer. If you can answer that you have, you can count on being reckoned quite a player by a person who thinks that a mashie is a kitchen utensil used on boiled potatoes. By the same token a negative reply classifies even a scratch golfer as a useless rabbit.

The odds against holing in one have been computed at between 15,000 to 20,000 to one. With one ace only to my credit, and having witnessed only one other, I reckoned this must be a gross under-calculation – until I undertook some research into the subject. At once I was staggered by the avalanche of hole-in-one data which descended upon me.

Obviously I had not been around as much as I thought, or I had consistently been in the wrong places at the times that mattered. And I was soon wondering whether there could be anything at all unique about any hole-in-one.

At first I thought the experience of Colonel A. A. Duncan, former British Walker Cup captain, of dropping a tee shot full pitch into the hole, where it became wedged between the pin and the outer edge of the cup, must surely be without parallel. Not at all. There are other recorded cases of the ball being played straight into the hole without touching a blade of grass.

Ah! He must be the youngest I thought, when I discovered

that in 1959 an eight-year-old boy, Brian McClinchey, holed out with a spoon at a 120-yard hole at Fauldhouse in Scotland. But soon I found that Peter Toogood, who has played for Australia in the Eisenhower World Team Trophy, was only eight when he had an ace at Hobart, Tasmania.

Ted English, one time county cricketer, was successful at Alton, Hants in 1946 in his eighty-third year. The oldest hole-in-oner? I thought he must be – until I found that an eighty-four-year-old farmer did the trick in Vancouver in 1954.

A blind man once had a hole-in-one at Pasadena, and as far as I could find he is the only one so afflicted to achieve the feat. In 1961 a certain John L. Knapp, playing his first game of golf, holed from the tee at Rochester, New York. Beginner's luck for Mr. Knapp? Not really. His tee shot from the ninth was so far off line that the ball holed out at the thirteenth.

One of the oddest aces must be that to the credit of a man at Ben Rhydding in 1953. He played his tee shot at a 190-yard hole to the back of the sloping green. As he was walking from tee to green contemplating a ticklish down-hill putt, his ball suddenly began to roll down the slope and finally trickled into the hole.

Here is an extraordinary course of events which must surely be unique.

Sixteen handicap Sir John Nott-Bower, former Commissioner of the Metropolitan Police, when playing at Royal Jersey a few years back, had a sequence from the fourth to the eighth, 6, 5, 4, 3, 2, then by all that's wonderful about this game of golf he aces the 120-yard ninth! His ball pitched two feet past the hole and spun back into it.

There have been a number of holed tee shots amazingly linked by repetition, sequence and common factors, stretching coincidence to incredible lengths.

Several players have holed in one twice in the same day and some twice in successive days. An assistant professional named McCandlish had two ones in the same round at Washington Golf and Country Club, U.S.A. in 1950. Another American,

Owen Moore, holed from the tee at the 125-yard fourth at Maplehurst, New Jersey, in each of three successive years, 1951, 1952, 1953, each time with a No. 7 iron and in the company of the same two fellow-players.

Three members of Sudbury, Middlesex, holed in one on the same day, and three players in the same four-ball at Shortlands, Kent, managed an ace apiece. Another case of shattering four-ball scoring took place at Los Angeles Country Club where at a 130-yard hole two of the four had twos and then the other pair each went one better.

What an experience Mrs. Paddy Martin had at Easter 1960. She played four rounds at Rickmansworth, Herts, and in three out of the four holed from the tee at the 130-yard third.

You may think it quite remarkable that two four-fingered players have holed in one on the same day, and that two players named Edward Chapman, who had never met, aced different holes at Richmond, Surrey, on the same day.

But more incredible was the day's double at Coombe Wood, Surrey, a few years ago when Eric Weisters and Derek Wadsworth, from neighbouring Maldon, holed in one. That each had an artificial leg was remarkable enough. But that was not all. Each also had a Swiss wife.

R. J. O. Meyer, Head of Millfield School, who used to play cricket for Somerset and was a scratch golfer, tells of a fifteen-year-old boy who declared his intention of trying for an ace at a fifty-yard hole. On the appointed day he duly succeeded – with his first shot, in front of about thirty onlookers.

Now for the contrast. An American in Massachusetts, desperate to have a hole-in-one under his belt, is reported to have hit 3,333 balls in one day at a 135-yard hole. Once he lipped the hole but came no nearer to achieving his heart's desire.

I do not know how often he had to clear the green of golf balls – nor how, after 3,332 failures, he still summoned the energy, and courage, to swing the club for the 3,333rd time.

A number of golfers have insured against having to buy drinks all round in celebration of an ace. One, an American named Priscilla Duckley, paid a twenty-eight shilling premium and qualified to collect £143 under the policy in ten days.

The Royal and Ancient, as the ruling body of the game, came to frown on this practice, just as they had deplored the popular custom before World War II of firms making gifts of golf balls, whisky and other good things to holers-in-one.

That they had reason for misgiving is borne out by what I regard as the most remarkable hole-in-one story of them all. The ace that never was!

The episode took place back in the early 1930's, and so embarrassing was the outcome that the facts were not allowed to leak out until several years later. Knowing as I do the source of my information, I am satisfied that it did in fact happen. But even after this long lapse of time, I prefer that the course on which it occurred be nameless and I will refer to the two key figures in the comedy-drama, as Mr. X and Mr. Y.

The day was either a Saturday or a Sunday and the Clubhouse was well populated at the appropriate time. Out on the course Mr. X and his opponent were putting out on the fourth green which is blind from the tee. Note that there were still fourteen holes to play. It is significant as a time factor for if it had occurred at one of the later holes in the round, the ultimate course of events would have been stifled whilst there was yet time.

While Mr. X was still on the blind fourth green, up came a ball from the friendly match behind. It rolled about a foot past the hole and Mr. X, knowing who was immediately behind and being on the best of terms with both, decided just for fun to knock the ball into the hole and explain the joke when the two pairs met later in the round.

In fact that was the last Mr. X and his opponent saw of the match behind and they wondered what could have happened to Mr. Y, whose ball they had knocked into the hole, and his friend. They were not to know that Mr. Y, on finding his ball in the sixth hole, was so excited by what he naturally believed to be his first hole-in-one, that he and his opponent at once called off their game and made haste back to the Clubhouse to proclaim it and celebrate in the traditional manner.

When in due course Mr. X had completed the remaining fourteen holes and returned to the Clubhouse he and his opponent found that Mr. Y had been celebrating for the better part of two hours and a formidable quantity of paper money had passed over the bar counter.

What to do in face of the unexpected turn of events? In the circumstances Mr. X and his friend, the only other witness to the mild prank, settled on silence as being the discreet course to follow. Later, to their horror, they learned that Mr. Y had claimed and duly received the usual gifts from manufacturers in recognition of his 'feat'. Whereupon Mr. X and his partner agreed that it was most unfortunate but all the more essential to keep quiet about the whole affair. They kept the secret for a long time and it eventually leaked out only when one of them blurted it out during casual conversation.

As the ruling body fears, there have probably been other fake holes-in-one. But as far as I know this is the only case where the ace was 'fixed' with no dishonest intent and where the true story ultimately revealed, was too late to put things right. Whether Mr. X should have confessed to the prank on hearing that Mr. Y had received 'perks' which were not properly his right, is a delicate matter on which I do not propose to express an opinion. In any event, Mr. Y had already unloaded his wallet at the bar before Mr. X had a chance to do anything about it.

Well, there it is – the best hole-in-one story I know among numerous extraordinary happenings which have followed a blow at a ball from a golf club.

But the holing of the tee shot, while often receiving extravagant acclaim, is not necessarily the most capricious of the golf ball's antics.

I can personally lay claim to having been the victim of one of the most freakish golf shots ever played. The stroke itself, at the short eleventh at West Essex, was most satisfactory in every way – until it landed, not on the green, but dead centre on top of the flag stick from which it rebounded high to the right and over the out-of-bounds fence. Playing three from the tee I took two putts for a five and lost the hole.

I can still recall the anticipation of a two as the ball descended by the flag and did not visualize the ball shooting off at a tangent when all seemed so promising. Just as vivid in the memory is the black look cast at an opponent who, taking the honour on the next tee, mumbled something about 'just one of those rubs of the green'.

Another stroke which I will never forget was played by a burly policeman whose sole desire on the golf course appeared to be to launch into every full shot with a ferocity which would have made Harry Weetman look genteel by comparison.

The occasion was an evening four-ball match of a purely social kind at Wanstead, Essex, between a society of which I was a member and a City of London Police team. We were one short, so the aforesaid policeman, a keen but raw novice, was loaned to us and assigned to partner me.

In the first three holes it was obvious that anything could be expected to happen when the lusty fellow took a club out of his bag but none of us was prepared for the fantastic stroke which was performed on the fourth tee. The Bobby actually contrived to drive out of bounds directly *behind* the tee! Lashing into the ball with uncontrolled fury, he managed by pure chance, to make contact dead in the centre of the club-face and the ball was away like a bullet. Only the essential elevation was lacking and with a thud like the crack of doom the ball hit the ladies' tee-box. The next that three startled people knew (I exclude the fourth in the belief that nothing on a golf course could surprise him), was a disturbance among the trees in the woods beyond the boundary fence behind the tee. That was the ball and none of us ever saw it again.

There is, of course, a moral to this story as there is in every case of dangerous driving, whether it be on the M.1 or the fourth tee at Wanstead. Mercifully for all four of us the sides of the ladies' tee-box were sloped sufficiently to ensure that the rebound passed over our heads – a safety virtue which any future designer of a new style tee-box would do well not to overlook.

It is claimed that at Westgate-on-Sea, Kent, a ball played to the short seventeenth, holed out at Victoria Coach Station, London. It was hooked over the hedge, pitched on to the main London Road, bounced on to the roof of a London-bound coach, and somehow lodged itself there.

Only a few miles farther along the coast-line, at Royal St. George's, Sandwich, what is probably the most costly of all freak shots was played. It almost certainly deprived Harry Bradshaw, at the time a little-known Irishman, of the 1949 Open Championship and all that goes with the much coveted title. At the fifth hole, Bradshaw's ball came to rest in a broken beer bottle. He elected to play it with a swing of his blaster, and his eyes closed. It went only thirty yards as what was left of the bottle smashed into smithereens, and he took six for the hole. Ultimately, Bradshaw and Bobby Locke were tied, after seventy-two holes, and the Irishman lost the play-off.

Truly we never know what lies in store as we line up the club-head behind the ball. Even the wildest of slices has been known to bring romantic results. Two delighted people I know became man and wife after a drive sliced by *him* had struck *her*, playing on an adjacent fairway. The profuse apology was accepted – and so was the proposal which followed some time later.

Sydney Spicer.

Ye'll be Needin' Your Baffie

My fund of golfing stories is limited but here are two which have amused me recently.

In Scotland the caddies take rare pride in their work and knowledge of the game. And they don't like too much interference from the players.

One dour wee Scot was caddying for a well-known amateur who was a bit wayward with his woods. So, at one of the long-shot holes, he asked for a 3-iron.

'You'll be needing your baffie,' said the caddie ignoring his request.

'No,' said the player, 'I'll be happier with the iron.'

'I'm telling ye ye'll be needin' your baffie,' persisted the caddie.

'I'll still take that iron,' insisted the player, and promptly hit a beauty that holed in *one*.

'Well,' yelled the excited player, 'what do you say to that?'

'Just this, sir,' said the caddie, 'you'd have been better with your baffie!'

* * *

Max Faulkner was talking to a distinguished TV star who had just become a golf addict. The TV star was seeking some advice and Max was trying to help.

Suddenly Max said: 'But what's your handicap?'

'Oh, about twenty.'

'H'm,' said Faulkner, pausing, short of a word for the first time in his life. 'H'm – it's not so much looking for what's wrong with your game, as what's *right*.'

Crawford White.
Bruce Forsyth (1st story).

Tale of a Dustbin

I am just an ordinary golfer, a member of an average country club in a small town in Huntingdonshire. I was once the victim of an unusual experience, however, which I feel is worth recording since it gave a good deal of amusement to the members of the Club and resulted in no small amount of good-natured leg-pulling from my friends.

I must explain first of all that my Christian name is Charlie. I was chosen to play in an away match, and, to save taking too many cars, arranged with a friend to pick me up. Early on the morning of the match I got my golf bag and trolley to the front gate and left them standing near the dustbin. (I should explain here that we in the country, unlike our counterparts in the larger towns, have to get our dustbins to the front gate ourselves ready for collection.)

Eventually my friend arrived and I went out to help him load, only to find to my amazement, that the bag and trolley had disappeared. So, also, had the contents of the dustbin, and I could only conclude that the dustmen had mistaken my tackle for rubbish. A frantic chase ensued to catch up with them, and when they were eventually traced, I found to my relief, that the bag and clubs were safely in the cab of the lorry. The dustmen explained that they thought they were too good to throw away and that they were, therefore, taking them away to sell! Inquiring about the trolley, the dustmen said it must have been shot out with the rest of the refuse at a previous visit to the tip. There then followed a desperate dash to the place where the rubbish was deposited and after scavenging about for a few minutes, the missing trolley was eventually found.

The climax to the incident came, however, a few days later. A competition was being played on the Club's course, and when the eventual winner was named, he was given the choice of either taking a small prize, or taking the key to open Box 13. (This had been specially rigged up for the occasion.) Sensing that there must be something special about the box, he chose to open it, whereupon two members came out from the secretary's office, carrying a large new dustbin on which was painted in bold letters 'PRESENTED BY A PROPER CHARLIE'.

Charlie Duller.

Real Progress

Lenny plays all sorts of games – mostly on me, I'm afraid – but golf is not one of them. He does, however, enjoy listening to a good golfing story, and whenever he hears one he passes it on to me. Here are one or two he has told me recently.

After a morning lesson from the Club professional, a golf rabbit played an afternoon round of eighteen holes. At the end of it he dashed into the professional's shop full of enthusiasm and gratitude.

'I just wanted to tell you,' he said, 'that you've done wonders for my game. I took ten strokes at the first hole, ten at the second – and I didn't have another ten all the way round!'

*   *   *

Smith sliced his ball from the fifth tee and it narrowly missed the head of a friend on the ninth fairway. 'I shouted "fore" old man, why didn't you duck, I might have killed you.'

'It wouldn't have mattered a damn,' said his friend, 'I took thirteen at the last hole.'

*   *   *

He also remembers with glee when he was in a Clubhouse and overheard the secretary and a committee member talking at lunch.

'I have had one or two complaints about the greens lately,' said the committee man, 'have you had any?'

'No,' replied the secretary, 'I haven't had any complaints about the greens, but two or three members grumbled about the meat-pie we had last Wednesday.'

Terry Hall (Lenny the Lion).

Candid Caddies

During a long, and very interesting, association with golf and golfers, I have found a particular fascination in stories about caddies, particularly in connection with the spontaneous wit which seems to flow so effortlessly from many of them.

My interest in the 'thirties, in fact, was so great that I collaborated with Charles Graves to form a record of their sayings. Our book on the subject was published in 1935.

In a Foreword to this book, Bernard Darwin wrote: 'That the caddie has an acute eye for human weaknesses no one can doubt, and this is especially true of the caddies in Scotland. Further, they can express themselves with a trenchancy that is positively searing. It is, however, I think, a mistake to regard them as deliberate humorists. On the contrary, they speak as a rule in deadliest earnest, and it is the fantastic and incomprehensible mind of their employer who finds in their words some mysterious humour. The late Andrew Kirkaldy was in many ways typical of the elder race of Scottish caddies. His remarks have been endlessly quoted, and he is believed by those who did not know him to have been a wit. Yet in fact, Andrew made few intentional jokes and his most famous sayings were, as originally delivered, ferocious in the intensity of their seriousness.'

Mr. Darwin went on further to say 'Caddies as a race possess a genius not for witticism but for brusque and penetrating home truths. Here is one mild little example. Not long since, I was playing at Addington and my bag was in rather a dilapidated and makeshift condition, reinforced by pieces of string. So after my first tee shot, which, I may add, was the very best of which I am capable, I apologized to my caddie for the bag and said I must get a new one. "I shouldn't do that, sir," he replied, "this one will last you as long as you're likely to play golf." That was a typical caddie's thrust, such as we enjoy when it is at the expense of our particular friends.'

Let me say now that Charles Graves and I would never have undertaken our book if we had possessed the faintest glimmerings of what was in store for us. It seemed very simple at the outset; for, like most of you, we had heard dozens of stories about caddies. They have been told to us in the pleasant atmosphere of the nineteenth hole with a large whisky and soda in one hand and possibly a 'chaser' in the other. They have been recounted in the correct argot, brogue and Scottish accent of the originals of the story. They have been accompanied by expressive gestures and with the still more expressive language of the original version. But oh, how they died on us when put into cold print!

We ourselves felt that if we racked our brains we could provide at least thirty or forty apiece, and if on top of this we acquainted the kindly public with our project – well, brilliant stories would roll in by the hundreds and it would be money for jam, for us and the publishers.

Full of enthusiasm we announced in the newspapers that we were looking for stories. We advertised, we circularized, we telephoned and we wrote for stories. We even paid for them in isolated cases. We interviewed, cross-examined, cajoled, browbeat, and begged Golf Club secretaries, golf professionals, leading amateurs, rabbits, humorists, women and caddies themselves.

We managed to compile our book in the end but it almost drove us mad. You have no idea what it is to read countless jokes on the same subject, however fruitful that subject may be.

From the start we made one rule which we did our best to keep. We tried to avoid all stories that were obviously untrue and unlike the real caddies we know. Such stories we considered were academically dishonest. So we confined our book to stories of what we knew did happen, and to stories that so obviously might have happened, that they simply must have happened.

Thus we savagely discarded this kind of thing:

GOLFER: Hi, caddie, isn't Major Pepper out of that bunker yet? How many strokes has he had?

CADDIE: Seventeen ordinary, sir, and one apoplectic.

There is no need to analyse this tale. Obviously no Major is called Pepper and nobody would take seventeen strokes in a bunker.

When day after day the postman staggered in with huge packets of letters we rubbed our hands at first, like delighted grocers. But we soon discovered some interesting but infuriating statistics. One story out of every twelve was that tepid chestnut of the Bishop who found himself in Hell Bunker, got out brilliantly with his niblick, whereon the caddie, with ready wit, observed, 'Mon, ye'd better tak that wi' ye when ye die,' or words to this effect.

One story in twenty concerned that old terror about the man 'who lay dead with his third on the green' with the inevitable retort, 'Aye, with surprise no doubt.'

Sometimes golfers who are playing for big wagers do not conceal this fact from their caddies, with the result that a certain touch of, let us say 'favouritism' is accorded to a ball by a caddie who knows that he can expect a bigger tip if he wins. There is that classic story of the caddie who, having 'scrambled' his man home, looks with disgust at the half crown tip in his hand as he soliloquizes, 'And to think that three times he drove off with one ball and ended with another.'

'O, pardon me thou bleeding piece of earth,' said Mark Antony to the corpse of Caesar. Sometimes the remarks of caddies upon the strips of turf that are from time to time removed by golfers, though not so elegantly phrased, are meant to be heard and sometimes they are not. The lad who, to the golfer's 'Good gracious, what shall I do with this?' replied, 'take it home and practise on it' probably muttered it only for the relief of his own feelings.

The brightest remark of this kind, however, was made openly to a reverend gentleman in the course of a round. Retrieving from a distance of about twenty yards a particularly large and bleeding piece of earth, the caddie inquired in respectful tones,

CADDIE: Shall I put this one back, sir, or would you like it for the Harvest Festival?

'Shall I put this one back, sir, or will you have it for the Harvest Festival?'

Here are a few of the stories we collected, and which we thought had some merit.

A golfer arriving at a very short hole on a strange course, took one look at it and was ill-advised enough to mutter,

'Oh, merely a drive and a putt.'

He topped his opening shot into the undergrowth in front of him, and was somewhat mortified to hear his caddie mutter:

'And now for a hell of a putt!'

*   *   *

A golfer having knocked out an enormous divot sternly orders his caddied to replace the turf. The caddie, thoroughly fed up after doing this for several holes:

'It is'na replacing the turf I'm doing – it's returfing the place!'

*   *   *

A retired business gentleman was being coached daily by his Scottish caddie. As he slowly improved, he promised the man a bottle of whisky the day that he broke the hundred.

After many weary days the caddie at last got his pupil on to the last green in ninety-seven and smacked his lips in anticipation. Unfortunately the old gentleman, in the excitement of the moment, hit his approach shot a great deal too hard and it sailed past the hole twelve feet beyond. Hard on its heels came the caddie as he dashed across the green, picked it up and shouted hysterically:

'You've done it, you've done it! Anybody would give you that one!'

*   *   *

This comes from Somerset and concerns a small boy who was carrying his first set of golf clubs. His employer teed up and then proceeded to go through all the various waggles, adjustments of stance, and so on. Whereupon the boy, unused to such preparation, suddenly said, ' 'Urry up, mister, 'it it!'

The other player immediately reprimanded him, but after what seemed a long time the caddie again broke the silence with: ''Urry up, mister, 'it it for Gawd's sake, I can't 'old me breath much longer!'

*　　*　　*

A caddie who was going round with a clergyman joined up with him at the side of a bunker and found him looking very worried and anxious. Standing on the green the caddie took off his cap and watching him the clergyman asked what he was doing.

'I thought you were praying,' explained the caddie.

*　　*　　*

A lady once played a nice approach to a high plateau green, and her opponent, a man, was bunkered in a deep pit-like hazard to one side of it. Her caddie went to the flag, and they both stood there waiting for the other player who had disappeared into the pit. Chunks of turf flew up, showers of sand, odd pebbles and so forth – but of the other player or his ball there was no sign.

The lady's caddie, beside himself at last, turned to her and said:

'Gawd, miss, he must be coming underground!'

*　　*　　*

GOLFER: I'll move heaven and earth to play this game properly.
CADDIE (a few minutes later): Well, sir, you've only heaven to move now!

*　　*　　*

'Sorry, you'll have to play that hole over again, sir. I got muddled in my counting, what with the church clock striking twelve and all!'

*　　*　　*

The Scots always come in for a hard time in tales concerning caddies, but as they are reputed to make up most of the stories themselves, we may assume that they do not mind. One, for

CLERGYMAN: Why are you standing there with your cap off?
CADDIE: I was merely praying, sir.

instance, is alleged to have inquired of his prospective caddie whether he was good at finding balls.

'Yes, sir.'

'Well, go out and find one now, and we'll start a round.'

*　　　*　　　*

GOLFER: You must be the worst caddie in the world.

CADDIE: No, sir. We couldn't 'ave a coincidence like that.

Henry Longhurst.

Take Your Pick

A golfing experience I shall never forget – and one which I certainly never expect to repeat – is when I holed out in one. You see, my handicap is the maximum a golfer can have. I did it with a No. 3 iron with a 205-yard drive, and at the thirteenth hole. It gave me added pleasure that it was at this particular hole and for a minute I thought I was back on television with Lucky Box 13!

A story? The following is one which I think is rather funny.

John Smith had been a very good golfer whilst he was on earth but he had not been very good at much else. When his time came, therefore, he was not very surprised to find himself down below. What did surprise him was that there was a magnificent golf course, and whilst he was surveying it the Devil came across to talk to him.

'Do you like it?' he asked.

'I think it is wonderful,' said John Smith.

'Would you like some clubs?'

'Yes, I should, very much.'

'Right,' said the Devil, 'come with me and we will see what we can find.'

They walked off to the Clubhouse where there were several magnificent bags of clubs standing in a row.

'Take your pick,' said the Devil, and John Smith went along the row and picked out a set of clubs which he thought were perfect. He had never imagined there could be such beauties, and by this time, he was itching to get out on to the course to play a round.

'They're wonderful,' he said to the Devil. 'I have never seen anything like them. Can I have a few balls now and get cracking?'

'I am sorry,' said the Devil, 'that's the hell of it – *there are no balls.*'

Michael Miles.
Cyril Fletcher.

Watching the Professionals

P. G. Wodehouse, a handicap golfer of some consequence, once wrote: 'Golf is in its essence a simple game. You laugh in a sharp, bitter, barking manner when I say this, but nevertheless it is true. Where the average man goes wrong is in making the game difficult for himself . . . a man who could retain through his golfing career the almost scornful confidence of the non-player would be unbeatable. Fortunately such an attitude of mind is beyond the scope of human nature.'

Beyond it, it is. Yet any man's success at golf depends very much upon how closely he can bring himself to a method in the game which combines the instinctive self-confidence of the old lady holing a putt with a reversed umbrella, with a relaxed simplicity of method.

In this, the professionals set him an object lesson in every tournament. How much can he take in from observing them? How much can he go back home and apply to his own game?

After watching professionals at work, one often feels that one has absorbed the movement and timing of it somehow, and that next week-end everything will suddenly become as simple as it is obviously meant to be. Strangely enough, next week-end it often is. But not the week-end after.

The influence passes, being founded merely on a sort of sub-conscious mimicry, not on anything that has really got into your head, nor into your muscle-memory. If it could be made less passing, and cumulative with repeated observations, then we'd really be getting somewhere.

I asked my local professional, Douglas Herd, what he would advise his members to try to pick up from the pros at the next tournament. 'Well . . .' he said, and thought for a longish time, 'I suppose it's smoothness, balance and keeping your head still. The best players all show a repeating rhythm in their swing, and they'll nearly always end the shot balanced comfortably on their left leg. So many amateurs, on the other hand, end up falling all over the place.'

'But really, it's difficult to say what I'd really tell them to watch – they are all different and need to watch different things.'

'But there's one thing,' he said, 'which applies to nearly every man in this Club. I'd tell him to watch the chipping. When they're faced with a chip, nearly all handicap players try to hit the ball up. If they really watch the pros, they'll see that every chip or pitch is played with a swing down through the ball and the hands slightly in front at impact. Probably that one point of technique, if he could really take it to heart, would help the week-end golfer more than any other.

'There's another thing which applies to all these shots. The pro may take a long time sizing up a shot – though most of them weigh it up as they walk along – but once they get ready and stand to the ball, they hit it with the minimum of delay. You won't see a professional nowadays endlessly waggling, or looking up at the hole again and again, or fidgeting about with his grip or stance. He knows what he is going to do; makes up his mind how he's going to do it; takes up his stance – and *wham*!'

Of course, with the best intentions in the world, the final

outcome of watching professionals, remains problematical. A tall, strong friend of mine, who was only then beginning to play the game regularly (having found that a cricket ball was suddenly moving too fast for his eyes), went to a tournament with the avowed intention of watching Weetman.

He came back with eyes shining. 'Doesn't he just *crack* it!' he said, and did a sort of swooshing movement which showed that at least he had appreciated the freedom of Weetman's enormous pivot.

The following day he set out to try it. He lost, in all, eleven balls, but still came in happy. Never in his life, he said, had he lost balls so tremendously far from the point where he had hit them – and two or three had gone straight!

It didn't last, of course. Nothing does in golf.

John Stobbs.

Outdoor Tiddleywinks

I am no golfer. Indeed, I once made myself unpopular by referring to the game as 'Outdoor tiddleywinks'.

McDonald Hastings.

A Ben Hogan Driver

I was in Australia in 1958 with the M.C.C. and we arrived in Tasmania early in the tour to play two games against the Island's State cricketers.

On the first day there was no cricket so the boys set off for the golf course at Kingston Beach, Hobart. Entertaining the side and myself, was Peter Toogood, one of Australia's greatest amateur golfers, and a four was made up consisting of myself,

Peter Toogood, Arthur Milton and Peter Loader. We stood on the third tee in a slight drizzle of rain whilst behind us the river wound in from the sea.

Peter Loader, then a long handicap player, watched three long drives sail up the fairway. Accepting the challenge he swung the club round his neck and topped the ball a few yards in front of the tee. He tried a practice swing and then went to swing again at the ball but as he did so, the club slipped out of his hand and went sailing away over the hedge at the back of the tee and into the river.

'Don't worry,' I said to Peter, 'that club was never any use to you anyway.'

'All right for you to laugh,' said Peter, 'but these clubs belong to Frank Tyson.'

A call to the greenkeeper for help brought the sad news that the river at that spot was thirty feet deep and the club was lost for ever.

When Peter met up with Frank later that night, he explained and apologized. Frank was very understanding. He listened and then said, 'That's O.K., Peter, all you have to do is buy me another Ben Hogan driver.' Poor Peter, Hogan drivers were then almost unobtainable in Australia and were the most expensive club on the market anyway.   *Alf Gover.*

Japanese Golf

A Japanese visitor was playing a round with an English friend and the latter was surprised to notice that every time his opponent's ball was not in a very favourable position he quietly moved it before taking an iron shot. Eventually he said, 'I say, old chap, that's not quite cricket, you know.' The Japanese visitor beamed up at him and replied, 'It's not the cricket I am a-doing – it's only the golf!'   *Hylda Baker.*

The Joy of Playing Golf

People often ask me if I get any fun out of playing golf and the answer is 'Yes'. I do get a lot of fun out of playing. Of course, winning big prizes is most important, for playing golf is my living; but if I were to think only of the money and worry about not winning when things go badly, I think I should climb up the wall.

Ever since I could hold a golf club, and that was at a very early age, I wanted to be a golfer, and that can hardly be wondered at because my father was a professional golfer before me. I used to listen with all ears when he came home from a tournament and told stories of playing with Hagen, Abe Mitchell, Sarazen and the rest. I thought then I would never be as lucky as that. But I have been, and I'm grateful for the chances that have come my way.

Playing golf for a living is not as easy as some people think. For instance, you are away from your home and family for long periods, and I don't like that nowadays. I can't get home quickly enough to Bournemouth, where my reception is always the same whether I've done well or not. The family is glad to see me. Then I can relax and forget the worries of trying to win one big prize after another.

The compensations? If you play well you make money. Then you are always out in the open air and you meet some great people, not only in the ranks of the professionals but among the general public as well. True, there are those members of the public who only want to speak to you if you play well, but they aren't worth bothering about. The others, the real friends, are well worth bothering about.

Then I just like playing golf. It gives me pleasure, and, just like a good workman, if I make a good job of it I have all the more pleasure. It gives me pleasure too, to keep on trying to improve. I watch other players and if I think their style can do something for me, then I experiment with it, adapting it to my needs.

Then there is the pleasure of hitting a really good shot, one that is perhaps better than any you have ever hit before. I'm still enough of a boy really to like hitting a huge drive down the middle. There is nothing quite like that for excitement in golf. And I'm not forgetting the thrill of seeing a long putt go into the hole just at the time when such a putt is very welcome.

No, it's the big drive for me. That gives me real joy, and I think it gives joy to any golfer. I think the golfing public like it too, for Harry Weetman, Dave Thomas, young Bobby Walker and, I suppose, myself also, draw a gasp or two if we really connect and send the ball three hundred yards or more down the fairway.

I know that when you go to a golf tournament and see professionals frowning and keeping themselves strictly to themselves, you may imagine we are a pretty grim bunch. But that's not true off the course. We have many happy evenings together swopping yarns and relating experiences.

There's no doubt about it, golf is a great life and I wouldn't change it for any other. But I warn any youngster who happens to read this – it's not an easy life!

Peter Alliss.

The Golfer's Wedding

I am much attached to the picture of the bride and bridegroom going up the aisle with a set of golf clubs slung over the bridegroom's shoulder, and with the comment, 'Well, it's not going to take all day, is it?'

*   *   *

A joke which is always a constant delight to me concerns the man who said his problem was not how near he should stand to the ball before he struck it, but how near he stood to the ball after he had struck it!

*   *   *

Finally, it always amuses me to consider that people who are learning to play golf have one big advantage over others in that their play sends them to parts of the country to which no one else ever goes!

Dr. Donald O. Soper, M.A.

A Useful Chip Shot

I always like a silly story, and particularly if it is clever. One such is the following, and it never fails to amuse me.

Two retired Army officers were on an expedition in the jungle. When they reached a clearing, one said, 'I've brought a couple of irons with me, old boy, it's as well to keep your hand in.'

With that he put down a ball, took out his No. 8 and played a chip shot. As he did this, a lion poked his head round a tree and roared. The ball chipped up and went straight down the lion's throat. The lion closed its mouth and the ball disappeared.

The other man picked up the club, put down a ball, and was just going to chip when the lion pushed his head out and roared again.

The first man turned round, and seeing what was happening said casually, 'You want this for a half, old boy!'

*   *   *

Another story I have always liked is this one.

Two golfers were standing on a green when a ball suddenly flew through the air and landed about twelve feet from the hole.

One said, 'We'll have a bit of fun here,' and with his foot he pushed the ball down the hole. At that moment a very sad-faced golfer walked from behind the bunker looking for his ball. Seeing the two chaps on the green he asked, 'Have you seen a ball?'

66

'Yes, as a matter of fact we have.'

'I don't see it: has it gone over?'

'No, as a matter of fact it's in the hole.'

'What – no, don't pull my leg.'

'We're not. It *is* in the hole.'

'Good heavens, you mean it actually came on to the green and rolled down the hole?'

'Yes.'

'Wonderful.' He then took out his score card and pencil, and wrote on it '24'.   *Arthur English.*

Ball on the Wall

Playing at Thurlestone in South Devon, in a mixed foursome with my husband, he made a magnificent shot, but unfortunately the bounce was bad and the ball landed on top of a wall. I was left to play an approach shot from the top of the wall. Held by my ankles, by my husband, however, I was delighted to put the ball only two feet from the pin.

Three holes later, we had the extraordinary experience of watching our ball being picked up by a seagull who, fortunately for me, dropped it about 100 yards nearer the hole!

Lady Isobel Barnett.

Golfers in the Dark

Golfers are a pretty crazy lot of people. Some fanatics will go to any length to play the game they love.

I was reminded of them just recently when I read of a golf tournament finishing in the dark because there were so many entrants.

Then, on looking through the records, I discovered there have been many instances of golfers 'being in the dark'.

Away back some eighty years ago, Tom Morris and Charlie Hunter, who, as local professionals, probably knew every inch of the course, played a round over Prestwick with two amateurs. The game started not long before midnight and continued in darkness till well on into the morning. Two balls only were lost during that frolic. Another nocturnal notability was one David Strath, who, in 1876, played round St. Andrews one moonlight night. His score was ninety-five and because of that David collected quite a bit of coin as he had backed himself to go round in under one hundred strokes.

Musselburgh links, too, has been connected with enthusiasts for whom darkness was no deterrent. Mr. J. E. Laidlay, who was later to annex the Amateur Championship on two occasions and whose short game was to become so superlatively good that medal winning just became a habit with him, went round the nine-hole circuit in the low forties in a game that started near the witching hour. He was a schoolboy then, and it is interesting to ponder whether Mr. Laidlay's skill, even on this occasion, could be traced to that overlapping grip of his which, at a much later date, became so closely associated with Harry Vardon. At Musselburgh's last Open Championship in 1889, many of the cards were totted up by candlelight after the players concerned had raced home in the gathering gloom. It was the extra brilliance of W. Park, junr., a 'local', that gained the prize on that occasion.

Artificial lighting on the greens made possible the finish of at least two important competitions which otherwise might have needed some time extension with its attendant complications – the P.G.A. Southern Section Tournament at Burnham Beeches in 1907 and 'The Craw's Nest' Tournament at Carnoustie in 1932. Those two flickerings, however, fade away into comparative dimness when compared with the dazzling combinations of electric lamps, oil lamps, car headlights and rockets that made light of the darkness when, in 1928, four members of the R. and A. played two holes long after the sun had gone to rest.

Hats off, however, to Mr. R. H. Locke, who, at Pannal in 1937, holed out in one shot with only the moon's light to show him where the flag fluttered.

It is very fascinating to read of the many punishing times through voluntary tests some golfers have set themselves. Stories abound of hole after hole being played continuously through daylight and darkness with only short breathers between each round. Moonlight, acetylene flares, candles, lanterns, flash-lamps, headlights, rockets and street lamps have all given aid to those who scorned the easy way to golfing fame.

To most of us, of course, playing in broad daylight is difficult enough without our becoming involved in the many extra trials and difficulties that would descend on us with the darkness.

Tom Scott (Golf Illustrated).

His Hole

A vicar was playing golf with one of his elderly parishioners. The old man won handsomely, and as they were walking back to the Clubhouse the vicar was looking disconsolate. 'Never mind,' said the old man, 'you'll be burying me before long.'

'Maybe,' replied the vicar, 'but even then it will be your hole!'

Derek Roy.
Kenneth Horne.

The Learner

Here's one story I like: Two women went into a big depart-mental store and walked up to the golf professional in one of the sports' sections.

'We are interested in learning to play golf,' said one of them.

'Oh, yes,' said the professional, 'I expect you want some lessons, and we shall be very happy to arrange them for you. Are they for you or for your friend? Or do you both wish to learn?'

'Oh, no,' she replied, 'it's my friend who wants to learn. *I learned yesterday.*'

*   *   *

And this is another: The Professional had a learner on the course for the first time, and before he began to teach him anything he said he would like to see if he had any natural aptitude for the game.

'Take a club,' said the professional 'and make a swing at an imaginary ball.'

The learner did as he was told and made an absolute hash of the swing. An American who was passing by at the time and saw the swing turned to the learner and said 'Say, man, it must have taken you years to perfect that shot.'

Lester Ferguson.

Allergic to the Game

I would like to help with an anecdote or piece about golf but the truth of the matter is that I am entirely allergic to the game. It is a curious thing about golf that those who play it enter an enclosed world with its own private language understood only by the initiated. If, like myself, you are not of that world, you can't enter into the fun, share the same jokes, etc. Perhaps, to twist the Stevenson line, lack of proficiency in golf is really the true sign of a mis-spent youth.

Frank Muir.

A New Player

One of the stories I like best is this one:

Three fellows at Sunningdale – very fine players, four, six and four handicap – were having coffee in the Clubhouse after a morning round, when a stranger walked in. Being a very friendly Club, and seeing he was lonely, they said:

'Would you like to make a four-ball this afternoon?'

He said, 'Thank you very much.'

They eventually all started off to the first tee and one of the members – four handicap – said to this chap, 'How long have you been playing?'

He said, 'I've only been playing a week.'

They all thought, 'Good heavens! We've done it now,' but, being good sports, they wouldn't back out and said, 'All right, we'll give you a stroke a hole.'

On the first tee he hit the ball about 260 yards, as straight as a die. He was on the green in two, down in three. It was a four bogey and with the stroke he won the hole. The second hole, a four bogey, he was down in four, and with the stroke, won that one. At the third hole, 160 yards, with a No. 3 iron, he was on the green in one, down in two. One of the members turned to him and said, 'I thought you said you'd only been playing a week?'

He said, 'So I have. *I was eighteen years learning!*'

Jack Train.

Anyone Seen That Dog?

The only humorous golfing incident I can recall is when I did a hole-in-one, playing by myself, and the only living witness was a dog! I called to him, but he took no notice at all, turned, and ran away. How about that for hard luck? Anyhow, that's my story, and I'm sticking to it!

Bruce Forsyth.

Scoring a Cow's-eye

Alas! I am no golfer! However, I was persuaded on one occasion in Jersey to go round the course with some friends who were very good players. We came to a small gully, and the ball had to be driven across to the green on the other side. One of my friends suggested that I should try my luck. There was a Jersey cow tethered in the gully some feet below, and I mentioned that I felt it would be advisable to move the cow out of harm's way. There was much merry laughter, and one of my friends observed that even I, the first of the novices who had never until that moment held a golf club in his hand, could not possibly hit the cow.

He was no prophet! I scored not a bull's-eye, but a cow's-eye! And the cow, quite naturally protested in a most vocal fashion, which brought its owner hurrying to the scene. He was flourishing what appeared to be a small sapling, and was obviously out for my blood. I left the scene very quickly, and have never been on a golf course since.

Bill Gates.

The Wrong End

A retired Admiral was seen once leading an injured player to the Clubhouse. In great glee, he greeted inquiries with, 'I shouted "fore" and hit him aft.'

Catherine Boyle.

Untold Joy in the Golfey

There is untold joy in the golfey.

Teedy-hup, swingit straight and left armpegger and falollop fair and far down the fairwayle O.digaroo. wristy flicker, contaps the ball and it's a hundred and or fifty fido.

Smart walkers or amblode, for here is a physicold and healthy in the walkit; and take a number several for approach and endeavry tock it on the green.

Sometimes it's folly for a bunkhole, and diggit deep sandy with a wedger or a lucky ploppen on the green for a putty in one or two and under bogey through.

Mind you, a richoshale from a tree trunk or twiggers whose droppy hazard cause many a lossy strokers and then it's profany language licence of the course permittit. Ts! Ts! (except for femold).

Other lossy strokers hazards are the copse, pond and gully Hup and down the whole creation, just over the hill and see the top of the pin and use a number eightloader. Finally, there is a sheer *joie de vivre* for the last straight powerfold and her-lob! As the eighteenth drive for a homeward. In spite of fluffy putte there is a great joy and a friendly chinwaggers at the nineteenth where many an armliftit for warming and cocklodes of the heart-strings and never felt better in my life!

Stanley Unwin.

New Ball

Here are two or three stories I like:

'Greenkeeper, did you know there's a brand new ball teed up on the first?'

'Yes, sir, don't touch it whatever you do. It belongs to old

Colonel Fotheringay. He comes out and has a couple of swings at it every morning.'

* * *

A beginner amazed his Club professional one day by beating him at every hole. 'I cannot understand it,' said the professional. 'Your game has improved amazingly. How do you explain it?'

'It is quite simple,' said the learner. 'Usually I wear contact lenses, but yesterday I lost one of them. The result is that with one eye I see a big hole and with the other a small ball. All I have to do is to hit the small ball into the big hole!'

* * *

A golfer came into the Clubhouse looking anything but pleased. One of his friends asked him what was the matter and he said, 'I've just been playing with a chap who says he is a Civil Servant. Every time someone shouts "fore" he sits down and waits for a cup of tea. I've come in and left him sitting there.'

David Nixon.

Royal and Ancient

St. Andrews is to a golfer very much as Mecca is to a Mohammedan. A player cannot really claim to be a devotee until he has visited the place, and it is therefore not surprising that, every year, thousands of golfers from all over the world make a pilgrimage to it.

Exactly when St. Andrews became connected with golf is not known. There has certainly been a connection for some hundreds of years, and there are those who are prepared to affirm that the connection goes back nearly a thousand years. St. Andrews is located on a rocky plateau several feet above the bay of St. Andrews and some thirty-odd miles from Edinburgh. The Old Course is the shrine itself but it is not exactly a heavenly paradise to the average golfer. Nor to the more accomplished player, come to that. It is said, for example, that when Sam Snead flew over to St. Andrews for the British Open in 1946, he took one look at the course and decided to fly back home again. He was persuaded to stay, however, and when he did finally fly back he took the championship with him.

Golf was popular in and around Edinburgh as far back as the early part of the fifteenth century and it took such a hold on the popular fancy that men forsook the practice of archery to engage in it. In 1457, it was decreed that 'the fut ball and golf be utterly cryit dune', but the enthusiastic Scots would not be 'cryit dune', and so at intervals of a few years, other ordinances were passed to stay the game – happily in vain.

In 1592 the town council of Edinburgh, jealous of the reputation of the Scottish Sabbath, forbade the game on Sundays. Scotsmen, divided between their allegiance to the kirk and their loyalty to the game, grew dour and sullen at the by-law. John Henry and Pet Royie, douce citizens of Edinburgh, were haled before the justices for 'playing of the Gowff on the Links of Leith every Sabbath the time of the sermonses'. For the same dire reason, Robert Robinson, of Perth, was seated on the stool of repentance in 1604.

For several years the golfers of Edinburgh and the golfers of St. Andrews were separate entities, and although it is apparent to students of the game today that one of these sets of players should eventually emerge as the leaders of the golfing world, it was not until 1754 that one of them actually did. It was in that year that the St. Andrew Royal and Ancient Golf Club was formed when 'twenty-two noblemen and gentlemen' of St. Andrews, met together and drafted thirteen articles to govern play. A century later the rules were revised and from that time they have been adopted throughout the world, except in the United States.

St. Andrews was granted the title of 'Royal' in 1834 by King William IV, and since then Royalty has always kept itself closely in touch.

To be captain of the R. and A. is to enjoy the highest honour in British golf. In the early days of the Club it was the member who won the Autumn Tournament who automatically became captain. Later on, however, the post became largely honorary.

The playing in of the new captain has always been something of a ritual. On the appointed day he steps on to the first tee, wearing around his neck a silver medal given to the Club by Queen Adelaide, in 1838, and makes the traditional drive. Strictly speaking someone should challenge the captain-elect but etiquette demands that he need play only one shot to win the match. When this shot is played, caddies take up positions on the fairway where they think the ball is likely to pitch – and there is no better judge of distance than a caddie at St. Andrews – and custom has it that the caddie who retrieves the ball is rewarded with a sovereign.

The majority of the caddies know the course like the back of their hand and he is a bold golfer who disagrees with his caddie's choice of a club. Caddies have been known to walk off when they have advised one iron and the player has insisted upon taking another. There is an interesting story of a caddie's help in the 1950 Amateur. Willie Turnesa was unlucky enough to hook his tee shot and find his ball in an awkward lie at the foot of an abrupt rise which blotted out all sight of the fairway and green. Willie's caddie merely handed him a 5 iron, and, pointing to the heavens, said dryly, 'See that cloud up there? Hit it!' Willie tried to do just that and was relieved to find his ball not six feet from the cup.

In the early years of the nineteenth century the Old Course was a great challenge to the up and coming players in a game that was rapidly becoming more and more popular. To go round the course in those days in less than one hundred was something like trying to run a mile in less than four minutes today. The first recorded occasion of a player taking less than one hundred strokes was in 1834, although, of course, it may have been done a few times previously. Later on, of course, in this century, Dai Rees was able to establish a record of sixty-seven.

In its early days St. Andrews had an interesting connection with rabbits. Some time around 1650 the Archbishop of St. Andrews was given permission to 'plant and plenish rabbits' on certain parts of the links. The idea was that the rabbits would graze the course and also supply the Archbishop with meat. Too much attention was not paid to the burrows made by the rabbits; these being regarded merely as additional hazards. Licence to keep rabbits was granted to other people over a very long period, but, as one might expect, there came a time when the rabbits did not seem able to distinguish between the rough and the greens, and the nuisance had to be eradicated.

All golfers are familiar with the nineteenth hole but few probably realize that it seems to have originated at St. Andrews some 200 years ago. In 1766 it was resolved that members should meet once a fortnight for a special match and 'afterwards to adjourn to Baillie Glass's house, each to pay a shilling for his dinner'. Later on meetings were held at an inn and it became the custom for members to bring along bottles of claret as payment of fines for various offences. A member who paid a caddie more than sixpence, for example, was required to bring along two bottles, and in 1839 it is recorded that several members were fined bottles for being disrespectful to the secretary.

G.J.M.

Down in Three

I must admit that I have never had any particular interest in golf. I shall always remember the look on Bing Crosby's face when he discovered that I lived less than one hundred yards from one of the finest golf courses in England and did not play. It almost ruined a perfect friendship.

However, I can tell what happened when I first went to play golf with Mike and Bernie Winters and had to spend the following two or three days convincing them that I didn't play. We arrived on the first tee and with a borrowed club, I did over a 200-yard drive straight down the fairway. The next chip went on to the green and I was down in three. They immediately packed up their clubs and refused to play any more!

Dave King.

Satisfactory Settlement

These are a few of the stories I like:

A little old foreigner was walking across what he thought was a common when he was suddenly hit on the back of the head with a golf ball. He stopped, and talking to himself said, 'Dis is a fine t'ing – walking in the country and I get 'it on the 'ead wiv a ball – I vill sue for ten t'ousand pounds.' Suddenly he heard a voice call out 'fore' and he very quickly replied, 'All right, I vill settle for four.'

*　　*　　*

Two players had just driven their respective balls, one well down the fairway and the other into the rough. The one started to walk on and waited for his partner to play out. All he could see was his head and a quick succession of violent shots. The ball eventually appeared and the ruffled player followed. His friend said, 'How many did you take?' and the answer came – 'Three.' Said his partner, 'But I distinctly counted eight.' Came the reply, 'So, I can't kill a ruddy snake now.'

*　　*　　*

An elderly visitor was seen to be starting his game when a helpful member of the Club went up to him and said, 'Excuse me, sir, but you are teeing up in front of the tee.' The irate player replied, 'Will you mind your own business, I'm playing my third.'

*   *   *

And here are a couple of quickies:

They were all square at the tenth, and so were the balls!

BEGINNER (to caddie): How am I playing?

CADDIE: Topping, sir.

BEGINNER: Oh, I thought I was playing badly!

Stanley Holloway.

Marley Spearman
The Making of a Champion

It is one of golf's most fascinating legends that a gay, young, London housewife one day passed over the fashions and the furnishings in a famous Knightsbridge store to take an impulsive first lesson at the sports department's indoor golf school – and little over ten years later was to have her name inscribed on a handsome silver trophy as British Champion. So Mrs. Marley Spearman took the first antidote to golf widowhood and the first step to a fame and popularity, rarely equalled in the often maligned, sometimes cruel, only rarely rewarding world of women's golf.

Slightly less known is the fact that after the one lesson at Harrod's Store, Marley went straight and signed on for a course of twelve lessons at the long established academy of Edward Boldright at London's Regent's Park.

Hardly known at all is the additional fact of extreme significance that those thirteen lessons are the only ones Marley Spearman has had. All the way from a thirty-six handicap novice to the British title, Marley has been a do-it-yourself disciple.

'Yes, it's true to say I have only had thirteen lessons in my life,' said Marley when we met in the bijou comfort of her

79

mews flat in London, W.2, only a par four hole's distance from the roar of Marble Arch traffic. 'After that first course of lessons I have worked it all out for myself. By continually hitting golf balls you find out where the weaknesses are. Mostly they are physical. A thirty-six handicap woman golfer just starting the game is terribly weak. That is her biggest handicap. The remedy is practice, practice, practice. This applies to any golfer, not simply the ladies you know,' the extremely feminine lady champion added archly. 'I had an enormously long swing when I first started and still had it when I was down to four handicap and played in my first English championship. That was in 1952, I think. Anyway, it was at Westward Ho! and I can't describe how weak at the knees I felt as I stood on the first tee for my first drive, and for that championship, my last match,' reminisced Marley. 'It is still the same swing basically today, only shorter and more compact because now I have more strength.'

Profoundly, the champion continued: 'I believe that the swing you are born with is the one you die with, so to speak. Whatever your method, it will work if you believe in it. I believe in practising all the time, but especially when you are playing really well. Then you are going to put really good habits into your swing. Having worked out a basically sound swing, practising is then not so much perfecting the swing as building golf muscle. Hitting shot after shot gives you this golf muscle.'

By this time a completely fresh view and a hugely increased respect of Marley was looming large before me. It was like listening to a book. The golfing lore and wisdom rolled off her tongue more freely than the pars and birdies from her golf clubs.

The general image of Marley is of the gay, London sophisticate, who, by an unremitting zeal for practice, had played her way to the top of women's competitive golf and at the same time had been so friendly, so completely free from malice or temperament, that she had won universal popularity. She was the ideal foursome player, the team player *par excellence*. She had piquantly turned the tables on her husband and mentor, Tony Spearman, had left him far behind golfwise, and reduced him to being a golf widower. The whole picture was gilded by her past link with the stage as a dancer. All this, of course, was more than the makings of any sporting heroine. Why should anyone want to dig deeper? Why, indeed?

The more one encounters the many good golfers and the very few champion golfers, the more it becomes apparent that a fine dividing line separates the two. There is an inner fire, a drive, a superior golfing intelligence, a firmer determination, a dedication, and motive, that together mould the champion. Marley Spearman hinted at, but did not dwell upon, the motive for proving herself as a golfer. It reached back to the days when her eyes were just opening to the mysteries of golf, when she first went into handicap competitions – 'I thought, how marvellous, you play the game for fun, and get prizes too' – and won so easily that the scarred tigresses of the ladies' lounge cast doubts at her being the novice she was.

Wounded Marley was counselled wisely by her husband either to quit the game altogether or get up and 'Show 'em'. We know the course she took.

It meant hour after hour of lonely practice on what she calls 'The Patch' at Sudbury golf course – where an indulgent head greenkeeper, Ken Eastward, made his contribution to Marley's progress by applying the 'Nelson touch' when she played practice shots to the greens. Two summers after her last lesson at the Regent's Park indoor school Marley had got down to four handicap. In another year she had won recognition in Middlesex County golf, and reached the last eight of the English championship at Princes. She ended the season by partnering John Atkins in the final of the Worplesdon foursomes.

The pundits were still sceptical about that long, long swing. They did not know that Marley was only just beginning to 'show 'em'. In 1955 England could ignore her no longer. It was the beginning of ever-present service in the home internationals in which Mrs. A. M. Spearman (Sudbury) met rare defeat. There were stroke play victories in the Spalding and Kayser Bondor national tournaments, three semi-final appearances in the English Championship, a dream round at Wentworth when a hapless member of the Continental team was ten down after the first round of Marley's début for a British side, and finally Curtis Cup selection. All these were the prelude to the coronation at Carnoustie, where the town provost paid tribute to the British champion, and to her victims, by saying they had destroyed once and for all that gratuitous remark of the Scottish male: 'I played like a lassie!'

All this time Marley was spending those solitary hours on the practice ground – and enjoying every minute of it. She said, 'I really do love to practise, just as much as playing. I still do, even now. It is never a chore and never has been.' This massive store of practice has always had a purpose. With the golf sense that earlier revealed such sound views on sticking to a basic swing, grooving the good habits, and building golf muscle, Marley went on to say: 'I am a great believer in hands. The hands and left side can't be strong enough. Hanging on to the club at speed is the test. A large part of my training is building up the left arm by hitting shots with the left arm alone. I would say that my first two years of golf gave me my basic swing. Since then it has just been a matter of building up more strength.'

Marley then went on to discuss the value to her golf of her experience as a dancer, at the same time making the point: 'Oh, I am so tired of this "former dancer" routine. I mean, how ex can you get? It is twelve years since I left the stage to marry Tony.' It is a point well raised. Marley's niche in the golf game is now assured by her stature as a champion, not by any curiosity quotient.

'I was keen on all sports and games as a schoolgirl at Wimbledon High; I went in for everything,' Marley continued. 'I started dancing very young. I suppose there was a competitive spirit to it, in that you had to pass the various grades. But it was the training in the use of one's limbs and the development of an aptitude for co-ordination and balance that proved the greatest help when I started golf. I remember Holdright telling me that the finest looking golf swing he had ever seen was a line of dancers in a show in which they did a golf routine. It was because they had been trained in the use of their limbs. Very encouraging to me, of course. Another aspect of dance training that helped, was the necessity for hours and hours of practice. My mind was attuned to it, and I knew how essential it was for learning any co-ordination movement of the limbs – as the golf swing is.'

Many are the facets of a champion. Marley made the further point that patience is a prime golfing virtue. 'Patience is a very good thing in golf. I have found it pays to be painstaking and methodical in making shots and in practice.' She makes no detailed analysis of her swing, saying: 'I like to have the feeling that I am hitting the ball squarely. The simplest way is the best way. To achieve it I say that the best thing is to work on the hands and arms and the rest must follow.'

Marley does not fill her head with theory. 'Tony and I don't talk it at home and the girls at tournaments and on teams, don't theorize to any degree. We confine ourselves to the idle chatter you would expect in any female gathering.'

Despite her enviable record as a match player, Marley's first love is stroke play. 'The greatest test is seventy-two holes medal. It is the finest of all training grounds. There you have only yourself to beat – and that's your sternest opponent in golf.'

On scoring she says, 'You are really getting somewhere when you can score well while swinging badly. It is your short game that can get you out of trouble on your bad days. And it all comes back to practice.'

Then was interposed a lament on the hopelessly inadequate

practice ground facilities at the majority of Clubs in Britain, a complaint that is being increasingly heard among star players who have travelled and enjoyed the practice facilities of Clubs in other lands. In Marley Spearman's case, she and her husband have done something about it. They have converted half the double garage beneath their flat to a magnificent indoor golf net, complete with side and rearview mirrors, mats, and channel for returning the balls. It is the complete workshop for Marley's golf swing. She defies the seasons and the weather. There is even a golfing 'punchbag', a loose roll of old carpet, about knee high, which Marley lays into with a battered No. 7 iron with such effect that the iron is now goose-necked. 'For strengthening the left side,' the champion explains. 'I can pop down here whenever I feel like it. It might be morning, afternoon or evening. I never miss a day. I play on Wednesdays, Saturdays and Sundays during the winter, always with men, off the men's tees. We play level and I manage to hold my own. Ian Stungo and Syd Scott's son, Alan, are often my opponents. Other training includes hanging from a bar, skipping and hand-grip exercises. A special one is hitting one hundred balls non-stop in rapid succession with the left hand alone. See that long wooden thing like a pair of sugar tongs? Tony or a friend tee up the balls for me one after the other. I really have to work.'

Finding this golfing gymnasium in the heart of London's West End, was all in keeping with golf champion Marley Spearman, the player with the infinite capacity for hard, painstaking effort; the champion who is quite different from any who have gone before her; the golfing personality who before our au revoir said: 'There is no secret to golf but hard work. No short cut. Just years of learning. And having a husband like Tony, who has been so terribly encouraging. You know, he doesn't come to the tournaments any more. He suffers more than I do. He did not sleep a wink the night before the final of the British. He gets as big a kick from my successes as I do myself. That is what makes it all worth while. That and all the charming people you meet in golf. Honestly, I can't say I feel any different because of my title. I still think "British champion?" Who, me? Oh, but I do feel that being champion in a Curtis Cup year is a tremendous responsibility. What a great age this is to be a young golfer, a time of wonderful opportunities to get on teams and go places – and now you can even cash in as a professional if you want to.'

Tony Spearman rounds off this tale of the do-it-yourself golf champion with the revelation: 'You know, I have given Marley every encouragement and opportunity to get on. I wanted her to have the best advice. I asked Tom Haliburton to have a look at her. Tom said, "If she has done so much by herself, then leave her alone."'

Tony and I agreed it was good counsel.

Ronald Heager ('Daily Express' Golf Correspondent).

Tramp Logic

An old tramp wandered on to a golf course one day and walked leisurely up the eighteenth fairway to the green. Having got there, he sat down, took an old sack off his shoulder, opened it out and took from it an old pile of dried twigs and two pieces of iron rod. He made the twigs into a small heap and fixed the rods to form an arch over them. Then he took an old tin can of water he had been carrying, suspended it from the rods and lit the twigs.

He was looking forward to a welcome cup of tea when someone stormed out from the Clubhouse and came running across to speak to him.

'What do you think you are doing here?' he asked.

'I am brewing my tea,' said the tramp.

'You can't do that here,' said the other, and in no uncertain language ordered the tramp to get off immediately.

'Who do you think you are?' said the tramp.

'I'm the secretary of the Club,' said the other.

'Well, let me give you a piece of good advice Mr. Secretary,' said the tramp, 'you are not going the right way about it to get new members, you know.'

Joe (Mr. Piano) Henderson.

No Patience

A young visitor to a seaside golf course accepted the offer of a game from a club member who was in his sixty-eighth year. Much to the young man's surprise he was well beaten, but he so much enjoyed the game that he suggested another on the following day.

'I'm afraid I couldn't manage tomorrow,' said the old gentleman. 'I've fixed up to play with my dad.'

'Does your father play golf?' asked the young man incredulously.

'Well,' said the old gentleman indulgently, 'he knocks a ball about, but I doubt if he'll ever make a player. He hasn't got the patience.'

Joe Loss.

Putting in the Hail

I was playing a single at the Albert Park course in Melbourne, Australia (this being my home town). The weather had been threatening all day, and we played our tee shots to the short twelfth under a sky of incredible blackness. My ball found the edge of the green rather a long way from the hole, and my opponent played a similar shot, also leaving himself a good ten yards from the pin. As he played his tee shot, I felt a spatter of rain, and as he replaced the club in his bag, it began to hail. We took shelter under a tree and watched the heaviest hail storm I have ever seen, continue for about five minutes.

When it stopped, we moved on down to the green. It took us some minutes to find our respective balls! They were almost buried under a thick carpet of hail. We were then presented with a problem. Obviously we couldn't putt through or over the hailstones, but I knew of no rule covering hailstones. We decided by mutual consent that just as one clears away odd bits of stick, dead leaves, etc. on the putting green, we would clear away the hailstones. But again, we knew of no rule saying how far away from the line of the putt we should move them. So we simply moved the hailstones a little to either side of the line we wished to take to the hole. Bearing in mind that they lay over an inch deep on the ground, you may not find it surprising that we both got 'twos' for the hole!

I find golf in England very pleasant. The courses are many and varied, and the same can be said for the golfers. The only big difference is in the greens. In Australia, they are watered more often and more heavily, and therefore, one can bang away at the green with no fear of running through. Even a 3 iron, if well hit, will normally stop on the green. In England I have had to adjust my short game considerably.

Barry McQueen.

Never Played Golf

You have put me in an awful spot asking for a golfing story. It seems simple, and I really would like to help *but* (and this is the plain truth) I have never liked or played golf, have never frequented golf courses, and, therefore, have never really taken heed of any golfing jokes. If it had been cricket, but there!

Eric Barker.

A Heavy Burden

Two elderly gentlemen – aged in fact, ninety-five and ninety-six years old respectively – decided to play a round of golf.

They got their chauffeur to take them to the course, argued about who was going to tee up first, but eventually – scorning a caddy as being a help for the soft young men of today – they arrived at the first hole. The ninety-six-year-old teed up, kept his head down, and was about to hit the golf ball when he suddenly dropped dead . . .

Some time later that day, the ninety-five-year-old arrived back at the Clubhouse carrying his friend. He put him down, and went up to the bar for a drink. Naturally he told the bartender what had happened, and shortly afterwards, a fellow golfer, hearing what the old man had had to put up with, went up to commiserate with him. 'I'm awfully sorry to hear about your friend,' he said, 'but I suppose it was even more of a nightmare for you having to carry him all the way back to the Clubhouse.'

'Yes,' puffed the old man, 'it just about got me down – having to pick him up, put him down, play my shot, pick him up, put him down, play my shot. . . .'

Jon Pertwee.

The Terror of Socketing

The transition from ecstacy to despair can be cruelly sharp and unexpected in most games. The bloom of a great innings may be destroyed by a second's lapse of concentration on the part of a batsman; the rugby player may have the line and victory at his mercy and then drop a simple pass; a jockey, with the Grand National and a life-time's ambition only a few yards away, knew the agony of frustration as Devon Loch sank beneath him. The hunter and the fisherman too, know the swiftness with which triumph can turn to failure, but of all sports, the most provocative must be golf, because the responsibility is the player's alone. No bowler is there to confound him, no opponent is striving to tackle, no horse can fail him and no temperamental fox or fish can tease him. The golfer is alone, his medium is inanimate and the measure of his success or failure is the exact measure of his own ability. There is no one to blame but himself, though heaven knows golfers are as ingenious as anyone else in their endeavours to prove to the contrary.

One of the most insidious refinements, and certainly the most humiliating of the various tortures from which golfers suffer, is the disease known as socketing. No other stroke can undermine the confidence and reduce a good round to ashes so swiftly. No other stroke is so universally feared. It chooses its victims with rare impartiality, for the socket is by no means a rabbit's stroke. In fact, it usually attacks those with some technical ability, and the man who approaches with a horrid little scoop or half top, little realizes how grateful the socketer often would be for one of those in exchange.

It is ridiculous that a man can drive long and straight, hit his woods and irons quite confidently through the green, and then be reduced to a tremulous wreck when faced with a straight forward little pitch. It is usually the easy shots which produce the socket because the player, in his anxiety to steer the stroke, probably fails to take the club back far enough or to hit through the ball. The result is an exaggerated roll of the wrists which shuts the face of the club completely and pulls the right arm away from the body and the clubhead outside the line of flight. Other symptoms are the weight falling forward on the downswing or excessive forward pressure on the shaft of the club, which brings the hands too far in front of the ball.

Golf is full of tips and hints to prevent this, check that, or cure the other, and the socketer will find no shortage of advice. Usually they act because the player believes that they will, but almost invariably, the effect is only temporary. As soon as the process becomes automatic, then other influences are free to begin their destructive work. Thus it is with socketing. The familiar remedies – stand closer to the ball, sit down on the shot, grip the club loosely, hit with the right hand and all the rest – often bring immediate relief and may even effect quite a lasting cure. But the chronic victim of socketing can never be quite certain. There is no ready cure for the fear and over-anxiety which are the basic causes of his complaint. A man cannot suddenly be unafraid and confident when his senses are trembling with apprehension. Perhaps caddies trained in hypnotism might help, but to be put under and brought round every time a promising socketing situation arose, would be somewhat wearing to oneself and one's companions.

I write from an unbelievable experience of these things, for down the years there has been much furtive removal of tell-tale white marks, not only from my short irons, but shamefully, from medium and long as well. I recall a time in the West Country several autumns ago. For some weeks the little shots had flown reasonably straight, and then from nowhere the socket struck. It always seems to creep up on one at the most unlikely and unwanted moments. A golden morning at Saunton was almost ruined; the matchless setting of St. Enodoc lost its charm in a fury of socketing and by Westward Ho! hope had almost gone. But in the depths of despair there came a gleam of light. Had not the greatest of all once been a victim?

Within the hour J. H. Taylor had confirmed what had seemed an almost blasphemous thought, and even now I can hear him saying, 'Hand me that mashie-iron'; as I did so he said, 'I was considered the master of that club, and yet for some time I socketed with it.' Humbly I asked how this could be and how could I be cured? 'Get your weight back on your heels,' cried the old man, almost pushing me over in his emphasis: 'sit down on the shot, keep the right elbow into the side, hit through the ball, and you will never socket.' Hope and confidence flooded back and soon I hastened gratefully away to spread the tidings. The next morning the sun, the sky, the larks, and the sweet loneliness of the links had registered their meaning. Never again I thought, as shot after shot left the approximate centre of the club, the socket is behind me for ever. The appalling optimism of this thought was not brought home for some time. Whilst confidence lasted one was safe, and then inevitably came the day when the ball lay a little tight and one was standing slightly above it. The unspeakable thought sprang unbidden to mind and the unspeakable stroke followed.

The awful thing about socketing is its unexpectedness. Suddenly, perhaps after months of relief, the traitorous thought, 'I might socket this one', comes to mind. Or a malicious opponent may whisper the dreaded word, as one distinguished lady golfer did with disastrous effect one morning at Deal. On occasions like this the mind turns prayerfully to the preventives, but as anxiety mounts, so does the body fail to respond to instructions. The weight is thrust back on the heels, the right elbow is tucked in and the club held loosely, but by now the wretched mind is astir with inhibitions. In the desire to get the shot over, one is undone and there is the ball, hurtling knee high to cover-point.

The socket is especially cruel, for invariably it costs more than one stroke. Even if recovery be possible, the mind by then is perfectly conditioned to socket again. From visualizing a pretty pitch nestling by the hole, with a possible putt for three, one is condemned in a trice to struggling desperately for a five or worse. And the whole performance is so ignominious.

P. A. Ward-Thomas.

No New Ball

A bad player who at the first tee placed a brand new ball down and hit it straight into a wood where it couldn't be retrieved, put down another new ball and the same thing happened again. He did this at least three more times, each time using a new ball. His partner said, 'I say, old man, why don't you use an old ball?' and the rabbit replied, 'Old ball? – I never have one!'

Brian Johnston.
David Jacobs.

A Lesson for the 'Rabbits'

A golfer who was an excellent player himself and who hated playing with anyone who was not first class, was sitting in the Clubhouse one day waiting for a suitable partner to turn up. No one arrived, however, and the only other occupants were three members whom he knew to be very moderate players indeed. They hinted two or three times that they would be pleased for him to join them but on each occasion he declined tactfully. As time wore on, however, he thought that any sort of a game would be better than none, and finally he accepted their offer.

Out on the course he soon lost his patience and got thoroughly fed up with the way the other three were playing. Eventually it was his turn to play a chip shot and he turned to his caddie and asked for his putter.

'But, sir . . .' began the caddie.

'I know it's unorthodox,' he said, 'but I just want to show these silly fools that anyone can play reasonably good golf with any sort of club.'

He played the shot and left the ball within a foot or so of the pin. His partner came up to putt it, muffed it badly, and sent the ball four or five feet beyond the hole.

'Give me a wood,' shouted the man to his caddie, and taking it, he putted the ball beautifully into the hole. He then went up to the hole and stood over it, calling to his caddie, 'Now give me a niblick and I'll show the blighters how to get it *out* of the hole.'   *David Hughes.*

Private Tuition can be a Mixed Blessing

It is not so many years ago that such a phenomenon as a private golf professional existed. Certainly I remember hearing my father speak of some, and though I cannot recall any to mind today, there once really were a number of rich and illustrious people who were great lovers of the game of golf and who, striving at all times to become more proficient at this fascinating and frustrating game, went to such lengths as to acquire their own private 'pro'. Many addicts of today still dream of this being the perfect answer to all their golfing problems and regret that a lack of wherewithal, or of time, makes such a proposition impractical or impossible. I know the feeling. I hear it summed up often when a pupil, catching on at last to the theme I have been chanting in at least ten different ways since the beginning of the hour, begins to hit a series of pearlers down the practice ground. When the expression fails to register delight and remains instead one of resigned despair, I know at once what is coming.

'Why can't I ever do it on my own? How I wish you could always stand over me!'

No booster for me intended here – just the old mental yearning for someone to lean on golfwise – the private 'pro'.

Many long years of teaching have proved to me that tuition is one of life's very mixed blessings. Like shell-fish, smoking and martinis, there just isn't a hard and fast rule as to how much you should take. Except, of course, enough to do you some good – and only the individual can sort that one out.

Take a look how much tuition the top players in golf take; surprisingly little. They have built the foundations of their game at an early age, possibly with the help of the club pro and almost certainly by modelling themselves on various heroes of their local scene. From there onwards, their tuition has come from within themselves – otherwise they wouldn't have reached a point of becoming great. I don't mean that great players never have someone to take a look at their game – I know they do – but it is coupled with their own thinking and is usually a matter of getting some confirmation. These players know their own game so well, that throughout the years they have been able to work out for themselves what they are doing – if it is good, how to keep it; if bad, what puts it right.

Today I find myself in constant contact with promising young players of mixed nationalities, all eager to learn, all anxious to apply. For some tuition is the answer to improvement – they have never had it or they need a solid foundation to work on. But even for these, there is a point of cessation – before they become lazy thinkers. Others have had a surfeit of lessons. They come to me over-taught and accustomed to leaning on the words of a teacher, and quite incapable of sorting out things for themselves. They must find it again by toil and sweat, trial and error, on the practice ground, until they acquire, if not always the remedy, at least a thorough knowledge of their own game.

A good slice of my living comes from teaching golf and after all the years I have spent at it, it is still a satisfaction to set someone off on a course I know is right for them to follow.

It is, therefore, strange that I write here not as an advocate for more teaching, but for more rationed teaching. My aim is to halt tuition being spoon fed to many young people until they no longer wish to think for themselves. Believe me, this is happening amongst many of our promising young players of today. I hope these words will encourage those who feel inadequate to do so, to think hard and experiment long, until they become, to themselves, their own best teacher.

John R. M. Jacobs.

My Friends!

My old friend Jack Benny has only had one ball all his golfing life. And now he has lost it. The string came off!

Bing Crosby and I play a lot of golf together and I have a small course at my place where we often play for side stakes. The only trouble is that when I win, I always have to engage an attorney before I can draw the money.

Not everyone knows that when Bing goes out to play he takes thirteen clubs and a stomach pump. After every bad shot he takes poison!

One little story I like is this one. A commercial traveller entered a client's office, dropped wearily into a chair and said, 'I'm a little stiff from golfing.'

'I don't care who you are, where you come from, or what you are selling,' said the man, 'I am very busy and don't want to see you today.'

Bob Hope.

The One Throw Game

One of the nicest stories I know comes from America where, I believe, they are always trying out new variations of the game.

A certain Club member was notorious for inventing new ways of playing golf, and on a par five hole he had hit two very good shots and was not far off the green. He then walked up to his ball, looked at his opponent and said, 'We are playing the one throw game, aren't we?' He picked up his ball and tossed it on to the green within a few feet of the pin. 'Yes,' said his opponent, 'we are,' walked up to the ball, threw it out of bounds into a stream and turned round, saying, 'but we never agreed whose ball we should throw!'

Another story I like very much is this one:

A husband and wife were playing in a medal-day foursome.

The husband decided to drive off at the first which he proceeded to do – a long swaging 250 yarder. His wife then stood up for her next shot, slightly frightened, played a bad one and the ball bobbled over only a couple of yards. Without a word, the husband took out a four iron and struck the ball just short of the green. The wife stood up, addressed the ball and knocked it right across the green into a bunker on the far side. Without a word, the husband played out and on to the green. 'Now, dear,' he said, 'just tap it near the hole with your putter.' She hit it ten yards past. The husband laid it dead with his return putt but didn't hole out. The wife missed a nine-inch putt by two feet and the husband holed out. Filled with patience, the husband said to her, 'That really wasn't a very good start, dear. We took nine for that hole.' Slightly piqued the wife replied, 'What are you complaining about? You took five of them.'

I can tell you one or two true stories about some of my golf colleagues. Here are two:

Harry Secombe and Eric Sykes were both in the same bunker standing side by side, and all those on the green could see was a frequent flurry of sand from both of them. There was another flurry of sand but no ball emerged, only the voice of Secombe saying to Sykes, 'Don't you think we'd do better if we stopped trying to hit these and started to sing "The Desert Song"? '

On another occasion, Harry Secombe, standing up to play fourth in a four-ball with his three opponents well down the middle, hit the ball an almighty wallop and sent it sky high about 250 yards. He looked up at it and said, 'I bet it will have a ruddy dog in it when it comes down.'

Cliff Michelmore.

The Iron-headed Breed

In a lifetime of golf reporting, I thought there was no facet of the game, no trick of the players or spectators, and no subtlety of the caddies, that was unknown to me – until I met Archie McAuchtonerey. Looking back, I suppose it was strange that I never thought something untoward about that season when Big Hiram Cullough won everything on the circuit from the American Open and Masters, to the British Open, and the Worplesdon Mixed Foursomes.

That season, some ten or so years ago, I suppose Archie was already in Cullough's employ. But his employment was so bizarre that it would have required a crystal-gazer to have worked out just why he spent so much time around the greens of every championship course from Sandwich to St. Andrews.

I suppose that when I first saw him in action I never realized what he was up to. I remember the occasion. It was on the fourth hole at Prince's in the final round of the £10,000 Tincture Toothpaste tournament. Hiram Cullough, the big professional at Workingham, was level with Harry Weetman and Eric Brown, the other members of his trio, with a straight race in for top prize of £3,000.

So far as I was concerned, it was just a question of how many shots Cullough finished behind Weetman or Brown. In any case, the Workingham professional – who was virtually an 'unknown' – had done surprisingly well in the early rounds even to stand a chance of carrying off big prize-money.

Weetman and Brown both missed the green. Cullough, who played his approach shot last, took what I considered an excessive club for the shot – a No. 3 iron – and powered the ball in his unorthodox style right for the back of the green. A cry of 'fore' went up when it became obvious that the ball was heading straight for the crowd and the 'jungle' of heather and gorse behind the green.

In the scatter of people, the ball struck somebody and, lo and behold, bounced back on to the green and finished four feet from the hole. I raced over, determined not to miss a 'scoop' if I could get one.

'Who did it?' I inquired of an old fellow who was creeping

back to his raincoat and coffee flask, as the danger was over.

'Funny thing,' he quavered, 'it hit that fellow over there – but I could have sworn that *he* hit it rather than the other way round.'

'What do you mean?'

'He gave me the impression of heading the ball. Perhaps he was just trying to get out of the way and instead, ran into it.'

I looked in the direction he indicated, and saw, for the first time, Archie McAuchtonerey. I sauntered over to the Scot who was watching the players unconcernedly as they putted. Cullough holed the lucky four-footer, and went two strokes ahead of both his rivals as they chipped and took two putts each.

McAuchtonerey was wearing a thick tartan cap – with a curiously large neb. He got up from the grass as I approached him and shuffled off to the next hole.

My office rang later in the day requesting that I hurry back to London to get to work on an Olympic story and so I missed the finish of the tournament. It was not until I picked up a late edition evening paper that I read the back page headlines: Cullough wins a sensational finish. Lucky 'header' by spectator on last green helps him beat Weetman and Brown.

The story went on to relate how lucky Cullough was when a shot apparently over the last green struck a spectator on the head and was deflected on to the green. The deflection enabled him to make a winning birdie three and get a shot ahead of his rivals.

There was a picture of Cullough shaking hands with the spectator whose head had got in the way of his bad shot – and turned it into a good one. I suppose I knew even before looking at the other face whose it was – Archie McAuchtonerey.

I cornered them both in a small bar in the 'Elephant and Castle' (I knew Cullough frequented it) two days later. They were half-drunk and they told me the whole story.

It seemed that Cullough had hit upon a notion for making

sure that his ball always finished in the centre of the green – when it mattered. Taking advantage of the modern habit of spectators to crowd tightly round important greens, he had stationed McAuchtonerey near to one to give him a trial run. On the first occasion, McAuchtonerey had equipped himself with a motor cyclist's helmet, and as Cullough's ball came soaring towards the back of the green, he had launched his head at it in real Tommy Lawton style, the ball had disappeared into deep rough fifty yards away.

'It took months of trial and error before we found a material soft, and yet pliable enough to stun the ball and enable Archie to direct it to within a few feet of a target.'

The target, of course, was the flag-stick.

I didn't use the story. My editors just wouldn't believe it. Neither, if it mattered, would the public. But the other day when I read that a spectator had got in the way of a shot of the new American star Franklyn Cassidy at Wentworth, I wondered. Could McAuchtonerey be in business again?

John Ballantyne.

A Major Distraction

A father who was an ardent golfer was sitting in front of the television screen with his small son squatting in front of him watching a transmission of one of the leading golf championships. Twice within a few minutes one of the competitors missed a comparatively easy putt, causing the father to groan. Then came a putt of not more than eighteen inches, and that too was missed. The father could stand it no longer and clipping his small boy's ear he said, 'Why don't you keep your flipping head still?'

*　　　*　　　*

Two members were playing a friendly game when, at the ninth tee, they came up to a foursome playing in a competition.

Against all the accepted rules of golf, one of the members went up to the foursome and said, 'Excuse me, do you mind if we play through? I have just received a message that my wife is dangerously ill.'

*　　*　　*

Two psychiatrists were playing a round of golf and one muffed his shot and saw it sailing away into the rough. As it settled he muttered in a frenzy, 'Nuts.'

'Don't let's start talking shop,' said his companion.

*　　*　　*

Coming off the first green, one golfer asked the other how many strokes he had taken, and on being told 'six' he triumphantly declared, 'My hole, then; I did it in five.'

He repeated the question at the end of the next hole, where-upon the second golfer said, 'Oh, no you don't, it's my turn to ask first now.'

Jack Jackson.

Making the Great Decision

At a certain stage in one's life one must either give up serious golf altogether, or turn professional. I made my decision at the age of eight and gave away my only club – a driver which I used for every shot – and have felt better ever since.

Michael Bentine.

Some Golfing 'Funnies'

Here is a sample of my favourite golfing humour: Is a golf scorer a *tee*totaller?

I was playing golf the other day with a little man about 2 ft. 6 in. high. He came on to the first tee and brought with him a tiny little golf bag. He took out a minute driver and a weeney little ball, then this tiny bloke teed up, drove off, and shouted down the fairway 'two'!

* * *

'I'm not playing golf with that McPherson again. The man's a cheat. How could he find his lost ball a yard from the hole when it was in my pocket all the time?'

* * *

DOCTOR: . . . and whatever you do, don't play any more golf.
PATIENT: And will I live longer?
DOCTOR: You won't live any longer – it'll just seem longer.

* * *

WIFE: Where have you been till this hour?
HUSBAND: Well, I've been playing golf with some friends, dear.
WIFE: Playing golf? Are you trying to tell me that you can play golf in the pitch dark?
HUSBAND: Oh, yes my dear, we were using night clubs.

* * *

'So you've lost your job as a caddie?'
'Yes; I could do the job all right, but I couldn't learn not to laugh.'

Peter Goodwright.

Bernard Darwin

(An Obituary written in December 1961)

With the passing of Bernard Darwin the world of golf loses one of its greatest figures. The loss is also severe to English literature.

He has been described as the best essayist since Lamb, and for fifty odd years it has been an honour to the game that these great talents should have been devoted almost entirely to golf. To say that he raised the standard of writing on the game to new heights would be wrong; before Darwin there were virtually no writers on golf. Let us say, rather, that he was the first man in this century possessed of literary gifts and a capacity for fine prose to turn them to the service of sport. Others, by his example, were spurred to follow, and if unable to equal him were at least able 'to give him a good game'.

He was for more than half a century Golf Correspondent to *The Times*. Trained as a barrister, his inborn love for golf gave him no peace in the Inns of Court. Although a fine player, his intelligence, industry and knowledge of golf would not allow him merely to play the game. The result was a feast of prose to the golf lover for fifty years.

His writings for *The Times* were not only confined to golf, his fourth leaders being amusing little gems of wit and humour for the connoisseur reader.

Perhaps his greatest contributions to golf were his books of essays on the game, gentle, amusing, but with flashes of caustic wit. It was in these essays that his violent entertaining partisan-ship for Cambridge and British Golf was fully revealed: this apparent prejudice has been criticized, but surely the real reason is that 'Bernardo' was too great hearted a man to be impartial, and too honest not to admit it.

Bernard Darwin, though a journalist by trade, was essentially a gentleman – heaven preserve me from the wrath of Fleet Street! Most of his writing was done in an age when it was easier to be a gentleman, a calmer, less rushed and nervous time, when even a daily newspaper correspondent born and brought up in an atmosphere of good breeding could retain it.

Let no one suppose that Bernard Darwin was not a good reporter to back up his superlative prose. His accuracy in giving the facts was a byword. He also had a 'nose' for being in the right place at the crucial moment at championships: this was a quality that was essential in pre-war days, when there was only one score-board beside the Clubhouse.

In his later years he was stricken by the worst kind of arthritis, which made him virtually a cripple. But until the last few years, he still managed to get to the tournaments he loved the most, the Halford Hewitt, Worplesdon, the Open and the Amateur.

For the last three or four years his writings on golf were confined to occasional articles for *Country Life* and *Golf Monthly*. Many criticized these writings as belonging to another age. They said that he was living in the past when he wrote about Horace Hutchinson, John Ball and Freddy Tait and other ghostly giants, in preference to the 'par-busters' and cheque-seekers of today. But surely it is forgivable and even characteristic, for an old man to write about the people and times he loved, rather than a ruder period which seems a little alien to his upbringing.

Well, 'Bernardo' is gone! Golf will not see his like again. He has had imitators before, and there will be others now how will wish to assume his mantle. Impossible!

F. G. E. Binns.

Five under Bogey

A man who felt he was in need of companionship decided to try and join a Golf Club. He was successful in being elected and when he met the secretary he asked 'When do I meet everybody?'

'Well,' replied the secretary, 'first of all you must have a handicap.'

'I haven't got a handicap,' said the new member, 'as I have never played golf before in my life.'

The secretary explained that he must get a handicap and as his golf improved, he would meet more and more members and thus gain new friends. The new member asked how he could go about getting a handicap, and the secretary gave him a card and said, 'Now go round the course and mark down every shot that you take. Don't cheat yourself, and when you come back, give me the card. I shall then have some idea of what you can do. Later on, members will go round with you and mark your card and I shall then be able to put three before the handicapping committee and get you an official handicap. You will then be able to meet your first partner with a handicap near your own and thus will start the beginning of many friendships which I am sure you will find in the Club.'

The fellow drove off moderately well from the first tee and the secretary left him to go on his way. Some hours later he returned and handed his card to the secretary who asked him how he had got on.

'I am five under bogey,' said the new member excitedly.

'Five under bogey?' exclaimed the secretary, 'and you say you have never played golf before in your life? Let me look at your card.'

He looked at the card and said, 'How do you make out that you are five under bogey?'

'Well,' replied the new member, 'I am five under that score there.'

'That's not the bogey,' said the secretary. 'That's the *yards round the course*.'

Arthur Haynes.

Plenty of Clubs

Two drunks wandered on to their course, took out their clubs and went out to play. The first one put down a ball and looked at it. After a few seconds swaying about he said, 'Gee, look at all those golf balls.' His friend replied, 'Well, you shouldn't have any trouble hitting them with all those clubs in your hand.'

Harry Secombe.

Some Advice for Would-be Beginners

Since the end of World War II, golf has been in a boom period. Many people are taking up the game for the first time, and consequently most of the old Golf Clubs have become over-crowded. New Golf Clubs are urgently required to absorb the ever growing golf population, but, unfortunately, very few new golf courses are under construction.

For the beginner then, there is the difficult question of knowing where and how to start. In most of our principal towns there are public courses which are owned and run by the local Corporation. These courses are the ideal starting grounds for the beginner. Most private Clubs are full and often have waiting lists, but if entry can be obtained to one of these Clubs, it can very often offer better playing and practice facilities than a public course. A practice ground is of great necessity to a beginner – he will progress more rapidly if he is able to practise and learn the fundamentals of a good golf swing before venturing on to a course.

What equipment will you need? The cost of starting golf is usually greatly exaggerated and very often frightens away would-be golfers. To start golf, most people will find that four irons – Nos. 3, 5, 7 and 9, two woods – Nos. 2 and 4, and a putter – are quite sufficient. A strong pair of walking shoes can have spikes fitted and then, apart from golf balls, the beginner is ready to take his first strokes. Obviously, as a golfer progresses, new items of equipment will be required, but to start the game a heavy outlay is not necessary.

Correct coaching at an early stage in a golfer's life is essential if he wants to make headway. A clear understanding of the correct grip, stance, and other fundamentals, must be gained.

A great deal has been done in the past few years to teach school children these fundamentals before they are allowed to develop faults on their own. The Golf Foundation takes care of this by employing the help of the local professional to take classes either on the school grounds or on the local golf course. For the older person wishing to learn, the Central Council of Physical Recreation runs a course of weekly lessons. These take place in the spring at courses all over England, and are run by a professional.

Intelligent practice is the quickest way to improve your golf. I do not think anyone would contradict this statement, but so many golfers waste hours of time and energy by practising the incorrect way.

Before going on to a practice ground you must have a very clear understanding of what you are trying to do. Hours of hitting balls aimlessly up and down a practice fairway will be of no benefit at all. Always hit your practice shots to a target – there is sure to be either a practice green, a house or a tree in the distance on which to aim. Aiming at a target will help in two ways. Firstly, it will ensure that the correct stance is taken up for each shot which will stop wild and loose hitting, and secondly, it will help correct aiming which will be of benefit when playing the course. To help obtain the correct direction, a club placed across the toes will quickly show where you are aiming when viewed from behind. Another club placed at a right angle to the intended line of flight, will help check the ball positioning – i.e. the ball is placed opposite the left heel for wooden clubs, two inches inside for the long irons, two inches farther back for the medium irons, and central for the short irons.

Here are a few exercises to try during your practice periods:

1. Strong wrists and forearms are essential in hitting a solid golf shot. To help develop these 'golf muscles' hit a number of shots without changing your grip on the club. Start with three or four shots and gradually build up to twelve. You will be surprised how much stronger your next shots feel after the exercise.

2. To train the hands to work correctly without excessive body movement, an excellent exercise is to hit shots standing with both feet placed together, shoes touching. This will also

help to teach correct balance and correct wrist action. If these shots are hit correctly, the ball will be hit to within approximately ten yards of a normal stroke. Choose a short iron to start with.

3. Hitting shots one-handed is a slightly more advanced exercise but is an excellent way to strengthen the hands and arms. About ten minutes with each hand before each practice session, is quite sufficient to begin with. Remember, the left arm is *extended* on the back-swing and down-swing, the right elbow is *bent* on the back-swing and down-swing.

The exercises so far are purely to help train the hands and arms to function correctly. The next one is to develop the correct co-ordination between the lower and top half of the body. The stronger the hand and arm muscles, the easier this exercise will be.

4. Use either a No. 5 or 7 iron and pace out a distance of about thirty yards short of where a full shot would pitch. Then gripping the club slightly down from the top of the shaft, practise hitting the ball to your target with a slow, full swing. No wrist movement should be felt in this exercise. Attention should be drawn to the co-ordination between left knee and left arm on the back-swing, and the right knee and right arm on the through-swing. Remember that this exercise is helping to obtain accuracy, do not over-hit the shot. The stroke must be played at an even tempo with the arms and knees moving at the same speed. This is an exercise, not a method of playing, although for shots into the wind, this is the method used for playing low push shots.

General physical exercises to help build up fitness can be used to good advantage by young men and women. Exercises which can be done at home include press-ups, skipping, and general arm and body movements. Weight training under expert supervision is most beneficial. A word of warning here though, remember that strong golf muscles must also be supple, do not build up big 'block' muscles.

Golf is a game above all, which should be enjoyed when

played. One of the most important necessities for this enjoyment, is to be companionable to play with. Do not hinder or interfere with your opponent whilst playing. A watchful eye on how better players conduct themselves on the greens and round the course, will be of guidance. Always try your hardest to win, whether it be in a match or medal.

To help in the enjoyment of the game, a knowledge of the rules is essential. Before venturing on to the course, buy a rule book and familiarize yourself with it. Always keep it in your bag.

The aforesaid has been general advice to young people wishing to take up golf. Naturally, there is a good deal more to learn, and here a professional is always willing to give his advice.

David Talbot.

Not a Bit Worried

Coming up the ninth fairway, a golfer was surprised to see a portly looking female sitting in the middle of it. As he approached he said, 'Excuse me, madam, don't you think you are doing rather a foolish thing sitting there on the grass? You might suffer a serious injury.'

'No, I don't think so,' said the woman, edging slightly to one side, 'I am not a bit worried. You see, I am sitting on a very thick sheet of brown paper.'

Another little story which has always amused me is this one:

A golfer and his wife were often quarrelling because he spent so much time at golf and so little time at home. One day, the argument got particularly heated and finally, in desperation, the husband shrieked, 'For goodness' sake, woman, shut up! You are driving me out of my mind.'

'That, my dear,' said the wife sweetly, 'would hardly be a drive, it would merely be a short putt.'

Stan Stennett.

Distance and Accuracy

A group of golfers were telling tall stories. At last came the veteran's turn: 'Well,' he said, 'I once drove a ball, accidentally of course, through a cottage window. The ball knocked over the oil lamp and the place caught fire.'

'What did you do?' asked his friends.

'Oh,' said the veteran, 'I immediately teed another ball, took careful aim and hit the fire alarm on Main Street. That brought out the fire brigade before any damage was done.'

*   *   *

St. Peter and St. Thomas were playing golf one heavenly afternoon and St. Peter's first drive was a hole-in-one. St. Thomas stepped to the tee and also scored a hole-in-one.

'All right now,' said St. Peter, 'let's cut out the miracles and play golf.'

*   *   *

'Well, you said I had to choose, didn't you?' demanded the husband, in bed with his golf clubs!

Bob Monkhouse.

A Painful Experience

I was playing at Edgbaston once with the Club professional, Frank Jowle, and things were not looking so good. In fact, Mr. Jowle was handing out a first-class hiding.

After one particularly devastating drive, I determined to get going. I swung – and promptly collapsed. A muscle damaged in a stage stunt at Blackpool had gone again.

Somehow, I got to the theatre, went on and played the harmonicas, but cut out much of my usual capers. Nobody

'Well, you said I had to choose, didn't you?'

in the audience even suspected I was in agony, and that off-stage I was flat out on the floor of the dressing-room.

Between the shows I went off for an X-ray and a brisk bout of massage. My spine looked like a sword fish but I would sooner be like any sort of fish as long as I could continue to play golf.

A story I like is this one:

Two golfers went out to play golf one day and from the first tee one of them holed out in one. He drove off from the second tee and naturally his ball fell some way from the second green. 'Damn it,' he exclaimed, 'I've missed it.'

'You surely didn't expect to hole out in one a second time?' asked his disgruntled opponent.

'Not really, but I was hoping you would expect me to. I thought it might help to lower your morale.'

Les Henry (Cedrick).
The Three Monarchs.

The Missing Badge

Strange things can happen in golf. One of my most amusing experiences came at the 1951 Ryder Cup match played at Pinehurst, North Carolina.

During the night preceding the start of the match, the temperature dropped about thirty degrees or so and was not far from freezing point. The sky was grey and a thin chilling drizzle of rain fell, for all the world like a Scottish hill mist. It was far from being a pleasant morning. Indeed, Ben Hogan felt the raw, damp conditions so keenly that in between shots he put on a raincoat. Most of the other players, particularly the Americans, were well wrapped up and garbed to protect them from the unseasonable cold dampness.

One exception, however, was Scottish born professional

James Adams, twice a runner-up in the Open Championship before the war. Adams was so undismayed by the weather – he had no doubt played often in similar conditions – that he went out without any waterproof clothing or even a sweater. He was in shirt and slacks, and with his shirt sleeves rolled up to his elbows.

Adams partnered John Panton, another Scot, in the four-somes. Their opponents were Sam Snead and Lloyd Mangrum. Although play began at eight o'clock in the morning there was a gallery of several hundred spectators to see the start, despite the inclement weather.

For the British side Adams had the honour from the first tee. This happened to be the match I decided to watch. I cannot recall now what took place at the first hole – I think the Americans won it – but I do recall that the second tee, from which Panton had to drive, was to the right, and back a bit from the first green. Almost everyone trooped over to the second tee.

However, Adams decided to wait at the back of the first green until the drives were hit. I did the same, and inevitably we had some conversation about the weather and conditions generally. I did, I believe, comment about Jimmy's serene dis-regard in his attire, for the weather.

Looking across, we saw the gallery beginning to move down the second fairway from the tee and we began to walk across to join them. Suddenly we were halted in our tracks by a rather formidable individual in uniform who demanded to see our badges. He was a ticket checker of some sort. (On occasion in the United States an organization pays a fee for the concession of charging gate-money, and then tries to make as big a profit as possible on the deal. I believe that something like this had happened for the Ryder Cup match.)

My response was simple enough. I merely flipped open my raincoat and showed the large yellow press badge that I had attached to my jacket lapel.

At the same time, however, the thought struck me that

Adams, as a member of the British team, probably did not have any kind of badge. He did, however, go through the motions of searching his pockets, though without any success.

By this time, Snead, Mangrum, their caddies, officials and spectators, were already quite a distance down the second fairway and, of course, Adams would be required down there to play the next British shot.

So, when I saw that Jimmy Adams was having no success in seeking a badge that may, or may not, have existed, I said, 'Look here, this is Jimmy Adams, a member of the British team. He's playing in the match that's just gone down the second fairway and they'll be waiting for him to play.'

The ticket checker was unimpressed. He merely drawled, 'He must have a badge or he doesn't get past me.'

Jimmy's searching of his pockets became a bit frantic, but still brought nothing to light. By this time, the gallery was a good 200 yards down the second fairway. Again I tried to remonstrate with the checker, pointing out that he was holding up play. He was quite unmoved, said so, and this time dangled a bunch of admission tickets that he carried, under our noses.

Feeling that this farce had gone on long enough I reached into my pocket for my wallet, determined to buy a ticket for Adams so that we could get on with the match.

Fortunately, just as I was extracting some dollar bills from my wallet, Jimmy plunged his hand into a pocket that he had already explored at least twice – I do not know what he had in it – and then, flushed and a trifle breathless, triumphantly brought to light his competitor's badge. So he did have one after all!

That was enough. The ticket checker, without a smile, waved us on, and we hurried down the fairway to join the players and spectators who were waiting and wondering what had happened to Adams.

And that is how the 1951 Ryder Cup match came to be completed.

Percy Huggins ('Golf Monthly').

High Tee

It is funny how some stories seem to stick in the mind for all time. I still remember a golfing story I heard many, many years ago.

A very rough diamond of a cockney who came from the East End of London, found one day, to his astonishment, that he had inherited a lot of money from a distant uncle.

In due course he bought a big house near a golf course and decided to take up golf for the first time in his life – this being in the days when a little pile of sand was used as a tee instead of the wooden ones used today.

He made his way to the first tee with a very experienced caddie who took a little sand from the box and was just going to place the ball in position when he turned to the cockney golfer and asked, 'Would you like a high tee, sir?' The cockney replied, 'It doesn't matter to you whether I like an 'igh tea or a late dinner – get on with your job and stick the ball on the 'ump.'

Jack Warner.

Only His Wife

Two golfers were at a tee close to a main road and when one was about to play his shot a funeral cortege passed. Immediately he stood to attention and took off his cap.

His friend looked at him in amazement and said, 'In all the years we have played on this course together, I have never seen you do that before.'

'This is rather special,' said the other, 'that happens to be my wife.'

* * *

Vicar to partner chidingly, 'I have observed that the best

golfers are not addicted to bad language.' His partner, 'Of course not – what the hell have they got to swear about?'

*   *   *

IMPATIENT COUPLE (to man idling alone on the fairway): Why don't you help your partner to find his ball?

IDLE GOLFER: Oh, he's got his ball, he's looking for his club.

*   *   *

SHE: Why do you play so much golf?

HE: To keep fit, my dear.

SHE: Fit for what?

HE: Why, to play more golf.

These are a few of the stories which I have always thought amusing.

Cardew Robinson.

Wise Worms

Three times I took a swing at the ball the other day and each time sent a sizeable clump of earth skywards. Finally I spotted two worms who were watching my antics and one said to the other, 'Let's get on top of the ball before this fellow kills us!'

*   *   *

Feeling energetic the other morning, I took a lusty swing at the ball and *zip* – straight down the middle. Then I started again – with a new pair of pants!

Dickie Henderson.

Francis Drives Himself In
(1951 – From the September 20th issue of *The Glasgow Herald*)

Francis Ouimet, of Boston, Massachusetts, drove himself into the captaincy of the Royal and Ancient Club at eight o'clock yesterday morning, and if the youngest child among the hundreds of onlookers lives to become the oldest inhabitant, he may never see a better tee-shot. The drive fulfilled to the letter, the club motto – 'Far and Sure'. It was straight on the railway bridge, slightly to the left of the flag, and if the caddie who eventually retrieved the ball had not beaten it down before it stopped bouncing, it would have finished a good 250 yards down the green fairway.

The caddies had stationed themselves – with a nice regard for the captain's ability – well beyond the road that runs across the fairway. But those who thought he would play a safe hooky drive to the left, and those who expected an early morning slice, were equally disappointed. The drive was everything that anyone's drive ought to be, and for a captain's tee-shot, it was of supreme excellence.

The captain, with a blend of caution and patriotism, used an American ball which, being larger than ours, is easier to see and hit at the hangman's hour. But the ball was not of the kind that may be bought in any professional shop; it was a special Walker Cup ball, bearing on either side of the maker's name the outline of a lion in red and of an eagle in blue, and for once the traditional sovereign was not given to the caddie who retrieved the ball. Instead he received, no doubt with the consent of the United States Secretary of the Treasury and the custodian of Fort Knox, a gold five-dollar piece encased in a plastic frame. Its nominal value is about £2.50, but that is to put a low commercial estimate on a prize of great worth.

Long before the captain made the stroke, which of itself won him two trophies of the Royal and Ancient Club – the Silver Club and the Royal Adelaide Medal – the crowds had begun to gather round the first tee. It was a perfect morning with not a drift of wind and the sun throwing the long shadow of the Clubhouse across the first tee. The cannon and its attendant were in position in front of the starter's box, at the tee-box a microphone had been placed to pick up the click of club meeting ball, and the crowds were lined up behind a rope barrier between the tee and the Tom Morris green. The inevitable dogs were there, but firmly leashed by cautious owners. At a few minutes before eight, the past captains assembled on the tee – Viscount Simon, Lord Balfour of Burleigh, Lord Teviot, Bernard Darwin, R. H. Wethered and C. J. H. Tolley, the last two, old opponents of their successor.

It was now nearly eight, and the central figures of the cere-mony came down the old steps from the Clubhouse – the retiring captain, Sir George Cunningham, the captain-elect, bareheaded and bespectacled, and the professional to the Royal and Ancient, Willie Auchterlonie, at seventy-nine wrapped up against the chill morning air, but spare and erect as a man half his age. He won the Open Championship in the year the captain-elect was born, but in all his long memory of the Old Course and the great men who have played there, he can never have known a more notable occasion or a central figure more worthy of being honoured at the home and heart of golf. When the photo-graphers, many American among them, had been accom-modated, Willie Auchterlonie teed the ball, the captain-elect had the merest twitch of a practice swing, and then, with no more fuss than he has ever displayed on the course or off, he swung with a grace and ease that belied his years and struck the ball. At that precise second, by a miracle of timing, the cannon roared, full-throated, and sharp enough to make even the wary jump, and the club had a new captain; another Medal Day had begun.

Not only did the captain begin the day in the manner befitting one of his reputation, but he continued the good work in the medal. Save for missing a shortish putt on the home green, he would have equalled the best score returned up to the time of his finishing the round, but seventy-six was, in the circumstances, a noble performance, and one that many competitors with half his years, and less than half his skill, must envy.

S. L. KcKinlay.

The Swinging Dustman

I am not a golfer and the only golfing stories I know have come from my old friend Ted Ray. Here is one I remember him telling me:

A man who had had trouble driving the ball was on his way to his Club to resign when he saw a dustman sling a bin on to the back of his cart with what the man thought to be the perfect swing. Three times he saw the dustman repeat the movement. He took out his driver to try a practice swing himself – but only succeeded in hooking the dustbin and tipping the bin and contents all over himself!

Kennth Connoer.

Golfing Gorilla

The owner of a driving range had a gorilla and once challenged the famous Sam Snead to a match – a match which drew enormous crowds. Snead won the toss and drove 300 yards down the middle and about fifty yards from the green. The gorilla, following, drove right to the edge of the green and Snead then played a perfect wedge shot a foot from the hole. The gorilla, arriving on the green and not really appreciating the purpose of the game, was given a putter and proceeded to hit his own ball another 350 yards!

A story which has amused me, although it has only a vague connection with golf, really, is this one:

Two golfers were about to drive off from the first tee when, much to their surprise, a beautiful woman, scantily dressed, leapt from the bushes at one side of the fairway, crossed it, and disappeared into the bushes on the other side.

The golfers were just getting over their surprise when a man in a white coat repeated the woman's performance. They continued to watch as another, and yet another white coated male followed. A further man, again wearing a white coat, then came struggling behind carrying a huge bucket of sand in his right hand. This proved too much for the golfers, who decided to stop the next person and find out what was happening.

'Well,' replied the next breathless individual, 'the young lady comes from a mental home just down the road. She has sudden fits when she tears off most of her clothes, climbs from the window, and runs away. The gentlemen in white coats are attendants at the Home. We have to catch her and bring her back.'

Satisfied with the explanation up to this point, the sportsmen were still mystified as to the significance of the sand, so they asked the attendant about it. 'Oh,' he laughed, 'that's old Bert, he caught her last time and the bucket of sand is his handicap.'

Bill Cox.

One Upon the Bore

I do not play golf, have no interest in sports generally, and possess hardly any competitive spirit. This, however, is a true story relating to golf.

Some time ago I accepted an engagement to entertain after dinner at a Golf Club in Glasgow where I was appearing in the city in a play. When I arrived I was buttonholed by the complete golf bore who, in addition, was very patronizing about the theatre in general and me in particular. He was the Golf Club's Treasurer and loudly told me, with a leer, I'd be paid right after I'd worked – 'in cash'. I said little, but got ready and did my act. The ass brayed throughout, trying to be funny and attract attention to himself. My act went well, however, and after it was over I had a drink and a talk with a very pleasant bunch of people. In front of everyone, he handed me my envelope. There was a silence and into it the clot dropped:

'Oh, by the way, Kossoff, are *you* a golfer?'

'No fear,' I replied, 'look what it's done to *you*!'

It was the squelch that the entire Club had been waiting for. I was cheered to the echo, and left happy.

David Kossoff.

Some Odd Stories

'This can't be my ball, caddie,' said the golfer, 'it looks too old.'

'Well, sir,' replied the caddie, 'don't forget, it's a long time since we started.'

* * *

Mr. Ralph Kennedy, who claimed to have played on more golf courses – 3,150 – than any other player, died in New York at the age of seventy-eight.

There is a story told of him which bears repetition.

On an obscure Scottish course he complained that the fairway looked all alike to him, and asked his partner: 'Where's the first green?'

His partner waved his club as he said, 'See that chap in front holding a scythe, he's giving the green its weekly cut.'

* * *

A woman's husband, who was an ardent golfer, died suddenly and she felt very lonely living on her own. A friend suggested it might be a good idea to get a talking parrot to keep her company and so she went to a pet shop to see what she could find. She explained her circumstances to the manager who said, 'It's funny you should come in this morning, madam; it so happens that I bought a parrot yesterday which had been in a golfing family for many years. If you wait a minute I will fetch him and show him to you.' He went to the back, brought out a lovely bird, and set it on the counter. Then he said, 'The ball's in the bunker again, Polly.' The parrot immediately crawled

GOLFER: This can't be my ball, it looks too old.
CADDIE: Well, sir, don't forget it's a long time since we started.

on to the bars of the cage and shook it fiercely for nearly a minute, all the time swearing ferociously. 'That's lovely,' said the customer; 'I'll take it. Nothing could remind me better of my poor late husband.'

* * *

'I shouted "fore", but those women down in front of me won't move.'

'Try shouting "three and eleven three",' came a quiet suggestion.

* * *

The rabbit swung mightily at his golf ball on its little tee and missed it completely. Angrily he told it what he thought of it.

'You're lucky, sir,' his caddie interposed, 'if you'd 'it it, it would've been an 'orrible 'ook.'

* * *

'How is your husband getting on at golf?' asked a lady of her friend. 'Is he improving?'

'Not really,' she replied. 'I haven't been able to allow the children to go round with him yet.'

* * *

'Does he play much golf a day?'

'Oh, thirty-six holes roughly speaking.'

'And how many without cursing?'

* * *

Sir Charles McAndrew once related how, when a woman spectator at St. Andrews was struck by a ball, she looked at the approaching golfer for apologies and sympathy, but all he said was, 'Please don't worry, madam, my match is over: I won four and three.'

* * *

The professional set the ball up for the learner on the first tee, showed him how to swing, and then told him to try. The learner took a mighty swipe, sliced the ball across the course, between two rows of houses, and out on to the road on the other side. By an unfortunate turn of fate it hit a motor-cyclist on the head and caused him to swerve. A coach full of people coming up from behind had to take avoiding action and in so doing, collided head-on with another coach and turned over. Two following cars could not avoid the accident and added to the pile-up. When the mess was eventually cleared, it was found that seven people had been killed and several others had to be taken to hospital.

The learner was still going round the course with the professional, oblivious of what had happened, when one of the members rushed up to tell him of the accident. 'That ball you sliced,' he said, 'hit a motor-cyclist on the head and caused a very serious accident. Several people are dead and others have been taken to hospital.'

'Good gracious,' said the learner, 'whatever should I do?'

'I keep telling you,' interposed the professional, *keep your head down and follow through.*

*   *   *

A horse in training at the present time and running over hurdles is named 'Maltreated', which seems a very apt name considering it is by 'Maltravers' out of 'Golf Widow'.

*   *   *

A writer wonders what happens to golfers when they are too old to play golf. Judging from some of the folk most of us know, it would appear they still continue to play golf.

*   *   *

Two golfers were all square on the eighteenth green and the last one to play was left with a putt of about eight feet. He lay on the ground and surveyed it attentively for some minutes, got up, went to the other side and repeated the performance, flicked off a number of imaginary worm casts, stood up and walked all round the hole surveying it from every angle. Then he suddenly snatched up his ball and walked off muttering: 'I can't stand the ruddy strain any longer.'

INDEX

Opening doors to
the World of books

**Book Tokens
can be bought and
exchanged at most bookshops**